RHINO 2018 is available for $16, plus
postage; back issues are also available.
To order, visit our website,
or send check or money order
to the P.O. address.

Our website features the Big Horn Blog, as well
as excerpts from past and current issues, events,
audio poems, poet interviews, and prize-winning
poems from our annual Editors' Prizes and
Founders' Prize Contest.
(See back cover for details.)
rhinopoetry.org

ISBN: 978-1-945000-02-7
ISSN: 1521-8414

CONTRACT MANAGER
Rochelle Jones

WEBMASTERS
Darren Angle
Matt Kelsey

INTERNS
Haley Cao
Samantha Seo
Morgan Sylvester

ADVISORY BOARD
Michael Anderson
Enid Baron
Paulette Beete
YZ Chin
Alice George
Chris Green
Deborah Nall
Julie Parson-Nesbitt
Valerie Wallace

CREDITS
Design by David Syrek
Illustration, "Champion Beast," by Tony Fitzpatrick
Back cover illustration by Tom Bachtell
Page number ornament by David Lee Csicsko
Production by Godfrey Carmona

CONTENTS

CONTENTS

EDITORS' NOTE

There is wonder and delight in *RHINO 2018*, to be sure. Just as there is goofy, slack-jawed, and subversive humor. And, of course, the issue is flush with imagination and linguistic artistry. But with titles like "Naked Bootleg and the American Distance" and "Being Caught in a Failing State," this year's poems also reveal the distinctly anxious tenor of our time.

Some poems seem to reflect upon the larger political context:

I walk down the stairs to the lobby where there are men with guns *saying they are members of the "Green Revolution." One knocks* *me out with the butt of his rifle.*	Austin Sanchez-Moran
How do you leave America? Pursued / in a show of strength *and conviction, blindfolded // for your own safety.*	Samantha Grenrock
I don't think we need to know what we're afraid of, / *but if you're afraid of something, feel it, / the leaving* *and its pushing-away.*	Bryce Emley
You spoke like pain from a jukebox. / The dairy went under. *The men sprayed / clean the floor they'd built.*	Bevil Townsend
A body and its spirit are trying to move forward / *only to be blocked by the illiteracy of DAs and the local news.*	Cyrus Armajani

At times, the anxiety seems almost apocalyptic:

Fall formed a nocturne / of drowning, the sun / *above like a god / saying nothing, white bending.*	Angie Macri
Will the smell of plastic be a pleasing aroma / to the Lord? *The singed hair and vinegar, // rotten eggs, faint apples forgotten /* *in their fields.*	Marci Rae Johnson

For other poems, however, the worry is more proximate and personal:

I hardly think I was / the first woman he loved with his hands / *wrapped around her throat, skin plum-dark, // capillaries* *like shattered cathedral glass.*	Jessica Lynn Suchon
One of our first lessons was learning how to fall, / our small bodies on *the hard-tiled floors in whichever church / we could convince to have us.*	Marlin M. Jenkins

Whether the landscape observed is broad or more intimate, a sense of confusion, of dislocation and fragmentation are often expressed:

There are loose threads everywhere.	John Randolph Carter

My head is a lake. All kinds of boat secrets floating around. Francine Witte
Some of them sunk to the lake floor.

I haven't a wholeness. My insides are a cormorant / Petar Matović
with a scarf around its neck.

Yet the poems do not end in submission or defeat. They remain exuberant and earthy
and playful, always full of curiosity and honest reflection about living in this moment.
In fact, a droll, wry or lusty humor emerges in many poems:

I grew up facedown / in Chicago's spongy suburbs. / Pamela Miller
We ate dinner every night at the Heap O' Beef /
and bought clothes at the House of Sad Plaid.

This morning I forgot / to write my affirmation 15 times. / Gabrielle Bates
Now I'll never destroy white supremacy.

By the time I get home the moon's submerged in ice / Eric Roy
but my wife is still awake and wants / mustard potato salad
in a Styrofoam container / I'm holding tightly with both hands.

If I weren't so close to it // I'd say something / Benjamin S. Grossberg
definitive about the plasticity / of men.

My lover says I am nothing more than a nine-year-old Rick Bursky
with a car and a job.

Finally, you will find a sturdy resilience and vitality in all these poems: a testament to the
power of poetry to interpret and even remake our understanding of our world.

See how the bodies shine. In marked places. The people. Nicole Miyashiro
Made of bronze. No single one identified. Not a single one
standing alone. This is not surrender.

I say joy is the real lone wolf, / a Yellowstone park ranger / Virginia Konchan
in khaki, answering to no one / but the sun and field.

It tickles / when you use me to imitate the violin's glissando, / Julia Armstrong
swoop out the pit of my square stomach / with your palm.

In *The Coast of Utopia*, Tom Stoppard observes, "It takes wit and courage to make our way
while our way is making us, with no consolation to count on but art and the summer lightning
of personal happiness." And yet, Stoppard continues, "[I]f nothing is certain, everything is
possible, and that's what gives us our human dignity."

Brandon Krieg's poem about discovery, "I Find Not Following," ends with the line, "to wander
not intending." That is our invitation to you. We are confident you will find in these pages
abundant possibilities and many small miracles of the lyric imagination.

EDITORS' PRIZES 2018

FIRST PRIZE

Worms
by
Erika Brumett

SECOND PRIZE

You Have To Be Ready
by
Amanda Galvan Huynh

HONORABLE MENTION

betty
by
Amy Bilodeau

TRANSLATION PRIZE
Hat
by
Dejan Aleksic
translated from the Serbian by Charles Simic

FOUNDERS' PRIZE
2018

FIRST PRIZE
Asking for a Friend
by
Abby E. Murray

RUNNERS-UP
Odysseus
by
Joseph Fasano

Amelia Earhart Folds Origami Cranes
by
Adie Smith Kleckner

Midden
by
Paul Otremba

In addition, we selected contest poems by the following poets for publication in this issue of *RHINO*:

Cyrus Armajani

Erika Brumett

Rosa Lane

Nicole Miyashiro

Brandon Thurman

Information on next year's contest can be found on the inside back cover and at rhinopoetry.org.

Bella Akhmadulina
translated from the Russian by Diane G. Martin

Paul

Five years old. Spoiled. So cowed, cornered.
Poisoned by candy. Lonely.
First they kiss you, then they shove you into a corner.
They beat you. Then they cry a bit; son, forgive me.

Taught wine. They drink: Mama, Mama's uncle
and Grandma's Uncle George—a stoker.
"What's this?" he asks, glancing at a book,
fascinated. He hadn't noticed the books.

Grandma lapses first into bravado, then into illness.
She probably drinks more than the rest.
We're in Kaluga but from her depths,
as if breaking into song, shouts Lipetsk.

No one to play with here. Unless you count me.
Total hide-and-seek. The lamp beckons me.
But what can I do? Listen: "Storm in the gloomy..."
Now sit down. Write: M-A-M-A.

What's all this for? Is it necessary? Right?
That clouds, storm, gloom hover over Paul?
But how trusting Paul is, how bright.
How sadly he writes: M-A-M-A.

Thus we two sit together on the white world.
I, with the black secret of my mind and heart.
So poems are what abandoned children are for!
I can't bear to read: M-A-M-A.

Bella Akhmadulina

This way the days flow by, a selection
of nightly moons falling from the sky.
Enchanting speech, native to him,
captivates and alters Paul's mind.

Everywhere Paul waits for me and roams.
And calls for Belka[1], though not once, never
has my auburn-haired namesake met with him;
her kinfolk are diligently destroyed here.

Like, by the way, all those dogs. Good little Paul
ever mourned their terrible deaths.
Our folk are widely inclined to beat and maul,
though they live in long-term meekness.

Yesterday I wrote. When "Belka!" was heard,
like the beast of the same name, my agile, poor
self hailed, I leaped up from the chair
friskily, and hid behind the door.

Hide-and-seek's meaning suddenly understood,
I'll recall that stare till the end of my days.
Through the crack, the grief of all children flooded —
older, absolving — in Paul's eyes.

Paul embarked on his sad path back.
In his wake, a whole army departed, bereft:
iamb, trochee, anapest, amphibrach
and with them, the dactyl. What's left?

---

[1] *Russian word for squirrel*

Dejan Aleksic
translated from the Serbian by Charles Simic

Hat

It's not easy to wait for
The head of right size

To hang from birth
In a window of an old shop
Whose former owner
Reposes under the earth
Eschatologically bald

It's even harder to be
A church bell made of felt
On the battlefield of thoughts
Cold as the fingers of a cashier
Counting small change

If someone does stop
Before the dirty window
It'll be only to eavesdrop
On the boy with the accordion
And to drop a coin

Into a hat turned upside down
To yawn at the sky

M. J. Arlett

Wake

The five senses are a lie I don't remember
being told. No mention of pressure, pain,

or how we know something is wrong,
a sullen lingering on the hillside in July

when the boxes are packed, boarding passes printed,
and our mother is waiting to pick us up in England.

In the half-occupied master bedroom, an incessant
robot is chirping. Distant. Not enough to disturb

my sister who sleeps wearing a tiara,
clutching an over-loved polar bear. Not even

enough to wake me, at first. Only when the abrasive
notes cut into the crevasse of my sleep

do I rouse, confused, and pad the hallway to the far
side of the house. I've come

to learn the body can enact what the mind wants
without permission, how maybe my father

more than anything wanted to keep his family whole,
the only way to do so

to sleep through the day
of our leaving. His big toe emerging from the white plains

of the bed, the grating alarm beside his head,
and little me, poised at the foot,

trying to determine if his chest was a watch
in need of winding.

Cyrus Armajani

No, Like This

There is a beat behind this line and the next
an angry tap of a pen by Bic
        against a wood table carved initials
of neighborhoods and names police think they know the way
        a one-year-old pretends to read a book.
Upside down and full of spit.
        A body and its spirit are trying to move forward
only to be blocked by the illiteracy of DAs and the local news.

A body is made illegal and its spirit
        they try to disappear
but a body's hands are too hard
        clenched in a perfect circle called square called sand
called justice called broken trial of unbroken man
        with a broke down beat behind him broken bars
he melted with the gas he bought at ARCO
on a night who refused to rain.

Julia Armstrong

Theremin Seeks Thereminist

I assure you, the small tank of me trundles easily
into the heart. Historically, we live a touchless life,
my many grounded-plate players and I, but
don't let that stop you; my electric voice spills out
willingly to fill the airspace between us.
Pitch hand, volume hand over rod and loop:
my arms are circuit-metal and motionless. If you
cut me open, you would see a rainbow ribcage
of radio waves, an oscillator organ or three,
the collapsed green lung of a motherboard. I hoard
your movements: each twitch of the pitch
hand translates as vibrato, itches along my speaker-
throat, my voice the 'o' in *home*, in *open*, in *holy*.
I speak in five-octave operatics, in horror-movie
soundtrack, the cold shallows in the still pool
of water. (I am also the ripples.) It tickles
when you use me to imitate the violin's glissando,
swoop out the pit of my square stomach
with your palm. I shrill with mechanical
delight. My wires spit sparks, shiver and fizz,
alight with synthesized pleasure. Play me, please.
No need to touch me—I'm already singing.

Gabrielle Bates

Everything is Everything

Things seem to come naturally to people
that don't come naturally to me.
At fifteen I knew how to be a parent
but not a sibling. My mirror neurons
are so overactive, I move my lips
when Homer & Marge kiss.
To speak even gibberish after sex
is to ruin something. This morning I forgot
to write my daily affirmation 15 times.
Now I'll never destroy white supremacy.
Alexa, play Blessings by Chance the Rapper.
Alexa, is it raining? If you're recording this
please tell the 45th president I wish he'd die.
Tell anyone who will listen. My exile outfit
is already in a pile, gray on the gray floor.
I zipper it off in bed & step out naked.
When I open the fridge, its cold gust
hits my skin; I open too & it leaves me.
Cleanliness is close to godliness & I
am the opposite of both. My husband left
a single egg with a note. *I'm sorry, darling.*
A track meet happened yesterday.
Good luck, brother. Outside the rain pauses,
sunlight hits the TV in a quick gash,
& I kiss the egg. We could all be kinder.

Pritha Bhattacharyya

Forgetting

whether the finger comes before silence
or after, like a totem, protector
from storm. whether you come from
earth or an open palm – decide, decide.
whether a fissure predestines the chasm, your
terrarium becomes your jungle.
whether crows risk entering an open window,
whether
windows prefer to keep shutters closed.
whether crows are birds or men,
whether black is a color or a noose,
not whether you are a window but
whether you crack –
whether your finger can push
past soil, whether you can pray
with one hand, whether
jungle crows fly higher without glass.

betty

your beau calls you betty
your name is not

betty
you don't remember

your name
where is your mother's

dusky dinner-call
where your certificate

of existence
down some dark

safe your mate feeds you
from his manly mouth his

bristlescritch! against you
o blank anonymous body

you begin to feel like betty
how you imagine

betty must feel
look at you

all monikered & mouthfed
you are so infinitely betty

Kamil Bouška
translated from the Czech by Ondřej Pazdírek

Garden

No one would believe in growth here,
    in sun's ability to unlock blossom.
Wintry shadow wrestles saturated greenery
    and lumps of dead soil, one over another,
choke life, roots and all.
At the center, a tree, a bright type stripped by fruit bearing,
                grows into the ground, its buds darkening.
At the end, a compost overflows a ruined fence.
    The proliferation of decay
                lures a new beginning.
No one would believe in the childhood of such a dreary place,
                in the joy of gulping the air,
which brings me ever back. When the wind mows the garden
                        even the weeds taste sweet.

Gazelle

teach me
the balance

between
two spheres

the weave
through

root & rock
& sky

when turbaned
soldiers

aiming AKs
come in camo

trucks
teach me

speed's secret—
the burst

to launch
from this

earth patch
to the next

record 12974.

—after Tarfia Faizullah

The nepenthe   stains my tongue / and she

pauses / to carve.   Still /   the sky sleeps.

Why   *has the moon hid*   *its face*   *from me?*

I can't give   *back*   *something*   *I don't know*

I've taken. Persephone   blots / my wound   and says

nothing   Tell me / what you know   about the body /

and I will tell you   how it too must   turn / against itself –

how it prays   for victory   / or to be filled / with arrows.

Annah Browning

Southern Witch Doctrine on the Resurrection

If I never resurrect,
I shall not be forlorn.

I'll get eat up by the red
slick clay that's colored

my hair since before
I was born. If I am never

born again, I hope the dirt
shall fill my head

with quartz-rock arrowheads
buried white as the stars

I rarely looked at. I rest
in hope that I will never rest

in hope. I've torn out too much
muscle with my teeth,

too much blood's run down
my legs, and I've laughed too

high and hard—I'd rather
die, I said once, and I meant it.

I'd rather not respond
to a single knock at my door

that asks if I'd like to go
someplace clear

and bright—my face is humid,
my hair a root storm rising

in the flood, and if they say
skulls are always smiling

mine's just saying, hey there,
hello, hi, look at my teeth

carving out my wet black cake
of leaves, my slice of old dark night.

Worms

It may be doubted whether
there is any other animal which
has played so important a part in
the history of the world, as have
these lowly, organized beings.
—Charles Darwin

Little tillers. Ploughs of night-
 writhe and gizzard. Eyeless, they grind
 through humus—through leaf tip, rock
bit, rootlet—burrowing tubal
 as the tubes they burrow. Dirt-
  serpents, vermicelli, bait. Hook-
   clowns, inchlings, doll snakes. Sectioned,
  intestinal—each a squiggle
of innard—a stretch of entrail
or colon. *Intelligent, unsung*

creatures, Darwin noted, *humble men*
 born blind and dumb. He kept some
  in the cellar, let a few loose
   in the drawing room, where he used
   his son's bassoon to test their sense
of sound. (Low flats, blown long, made them twine
with squirm.) Outside, he tossed cinders
 on lime, charred marl on ashes, watched
  as earth swallowed earth by way of worm-
   work. As all was churned, pulled down. Stone-

henge rose from snow *like stacked bones*
that winter, when Darwin knelt—
in his final year—in its circle's center.
When he bent his beard over a slab
of fallen sarsen, sunken under worm
cast and loam that had frozen.
To know them before going below
to join them. Their ganglions and five hearts.
Their slow, slow force—aerating,
burying—alive with decay.

Rick Bursky

This, Too,
Is Harmony

X-rays revealed cave paintings inside my skull. I know what you're thinking,
the same thing the doctors thought, I find meaning where there is none …
in a brain that is a make-believe landscape impersonating a world. In a forest
in North Carolina I found a Civil War belt buckle and human bones,
a metacarpal and distal phalange; the belt buckle
from the 2nd North Carolina Volunteer Mounted Infantry Regiment.
One collector offered me eighty-seven dollars for the belt buckle.
What I know to be cave paintings doctors believe are the bone's natural creases.

Have you ever seen bees leave a hive on a summer morning
before heat takes the dew from the grass? I saw them — a dark wisp
in the distance straining between choreography and cacophony
— while digging that hole on the edge of the woods.
I slice bread with my tongue, tie my shoelaces with one hand,
keep my eyes open without blinking for five more than five minutes if I stare at my feet.
My lover says I am nothing more than a nine-year-old with a car and a job.

How angry the soldier would be if I offered him eighty-seven dollars
when he returned to claim his belt buckle. My lover says
coincidence is a clown in a sequin vest. I say fate, always formal, wears a dark suit.
The soldier would have said the eighty-seven dollars was blood money.
One of the cave paintings is of a stick figure of a man lying beside a hole.
A line of soldiers approaches him, swarming from the forest like a colony of ants;
helter-skelter to the uninformed, rectitude to the misinformed.
I'm a machine as much as a person. The truth is stunning.

What Is An Entanglement

Evan arrived into my life a tender blessing. Like an art gallery in a cave, a whole herd
Of deer in my kitchen, a lady chanting prayers at her home burning down, tinting
The gray sky a shade of orange, it was not so much his image, his particular collage

Of nose and mouth and hair color, much like the one who birthed him. As lovely as others,
As bitterly metamorphosing. It was first his voice, the darling sound he made when soup
Became available, as natural as any. It was second how he danced across the yard.

He made no gripe of the world and its offerings, its deliriums and decisions.
He did not bother the blue egg glowing in the passing grass like a child lost from its mother.
He did not trouble the field filling up with the circumference of geese. When the desire

To make bracelets rose in him, he noted our last twenty-six blades of grass and moseyed
Onward. He was the child who knew the dirt's last speck of hope, the geese's
Honking wish to be left alone. In his elementary school plays, he was the one

Brave child who always volunteered to play the old lady. He once brought me his two hands
Cupped around a broken egg and asked me if there was anything we could do.

John Randolph Carter

Threads of Imperfection

Life is like Nancy and Sluggo.
There are threads of imperfection in every utterance.

Where are the dishwashers?
Where are the windshield wipers?

Sad but inebriated librarians are spilling coffee on my thesaurus.

Men with long hoses and free time are circling my house.
Market forces are trying to force open my front door.

It's too late for supper and too early for breakfast.

There are loose threads everywhere.
Who can make sense of them?

Either my legs are too short or this horse is too tall.
Please help me find my stirrups.

Where is the fly in the ointment?
Where are the mints on the pillow?
Why does the parrot fish keep repeating my name?

Aunt Panties appears with her entourage of whistling gypsies.
Mandolins begin to play.
The audience files in, filling the seats with a puffy fluff.

Before too long the Emperor of Ty-D-Bols appears
and commands everyone to sit.
He sings in a whisper-thin voice.
Everyone leans forward, straining to hear:

"Come close to the fire, but not too close.
Develop an affinity for infinity.
Laugh, then cry. Live, then die.
Take a nap, nap, nap, nap, nap."

Susana H. Case

#8

—from Erasure, Syria

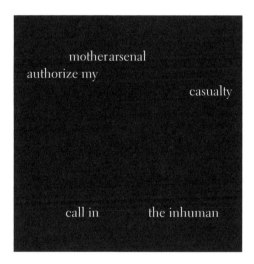

Gangsters, Disciples

—for R. Dotse

Beloved, you take me there: hold me down,
cuff me if I like it, the bad boy's punishment

or the black's. Your daddy is white, but what
does that suggest for the roses at my funeral

or yours? What shade of grief would they be?
Colors matter around here; we are symmetrical

in our patterns and pains. While you lay there
bleeding, I hold your hand and pour out a little

Lillet for you. Half of the time you hate me
enough to lay hands on me; we come to blows

because it feels good and let live. Bless those
broken homes that rubber-banded us together,

baptized us in dust and danger never knowing
when to pull out of a dicey situation. And so

I wipe the blade clean after it's made ribbons
of the flesh; you remain ready to take that heat

for me, handle product. We both have records
we're running from like errant needles. I know

we're on probation: it may come down to you
or me and a real gangster must choose themself.

Geet Chaturvedi
translated from the Hindi by Anita Gopalan

Collective Autobiography

*A time to be born, and a time
to die; a time to plant, and a
time to pluck up that which
is planted*
—Ecclesiastes 3:2

We are, like the invisible seeds buried underground,
waiting for water.
An old soldier keeps us in a cupboard
like empty cartridges collected from the battlefield.
We jangle
like loose change kept in pocket while sprinting.
We are the buttons sewn on a shirt
without the buttonholes.
We are the others. The etceteras. The elsewheres.
The *namaste* that was never reciprocated.
We are the torn innerwear of our nattily dressed times.
We will be told to rest in the shade of our own shadow.
Anyone who peeps into our eyes will sight
posters of giant waterfalls.
Our bodies will become tourist attractions.
In our wombs tourists will throw their litter.
One day we will say we are naked.
And the king will think we have called him naked.
He will lash our backs with a whip.
From the open wounds, flowers will blossom.
The king will be conferred the title 'God's most favourite gardener.'
And we will be offered to some idol in a temple.
Wearing a smile, the dot on which we end—
our poem will begin once again from there.
We will again become the invisible seeds.

The earth will limn the narrative of our growth.
Strumming on his iktara, an ascetic will sing our tale
on the ghats of some holy river.
We will float like lit oil lamps
by its shore.

Albert DeGenova

A Day's Work

He chews a black Italian cheroot
tight in his determined bite
a stiff-legged limp doesn't slow
his steady stride down the alley,
across Grand Ave, across
the tracks to a small patch
of park, to the west-facing bench
where he sits (sometimes he turns
away from the spray of the fountain)
and sits, a hand on each knee,
back straight, no slouch. I imagine
he listens to the falling water, this seeming
ancient pond, and hears the city
syncopation of hard-clanging crossing gate
bells, the rumble
of speeding commuter trains.
I do not yet know this kind of work.
He stares where there are no frogs
jumping in. How long he labors
inside this silence, so much living
in this sitting. Remembering –
          like lighting his cigar in the wind
match after match after match.

Bryce Emley

[poem written for my mother to say to me]

The weather is quiet here.
Lightning stitches the sky
back together.
The trees are oil paintings of fire.
What are you afraid of,
if not that kind of quiet?
When everything was going wrong
and you said your dreams were silent films
from other counties,
I was still homesick in my own skin,
a fever burning a house into the ground.
I thought I'd remember this much better.
Isn't that what it's always like?
When you were young, a bee landed on your arm
and you told me you could feel the wind
from its wings when it left.
I don't think we need to know what we're afraid of,
but if you're afraid of something, feel it,
the leaving and its pushing-away.

E. J. Evans

1174 Dryden Road

On the day we moved in together we planted a red maple.
It was June and bright and we were open to the world.
Moving through the house, feeling its spaces,
I sensed everything already changing under the surface,
that we were but objects loose in our respective currents.
Later, on days when the sky turned dark gray
and the clouds leaned down,
to look out of the back window into the yard
and see the path the wind made through trees and tall grass
was to see my own life made visible. There were no fences.
At any time I could have let myself go,
could have walked out the back door, through the yard
and out into the woods, and kept walking.

Odysseus

Think of the moment before the moment.
Before recognition. Before the nurse saw
the boar's scar coursing down his thigh
where the world had first entered him
in the forests of childhood. Before
Penelope. Before his battle for her heart.
Think of his moment alone on the beach,
his sailors running up to the village
where girls stood wringing spices
from their hair. Think of the gods saying to him
you do not have to praise ruin anymore;
you do not have to praise what is lost.
How you imagine him is how you enter things.
He is kneeling. Or he is weeping. Or he is turning
toward the sea again, thinking of the great deeds
of the hopeless. Think of him lifting the sands
and touching them to his tongue, to see
if it is real. If it is home. If it is time. Think of the moment
before he knew he had stepped out of the myths
and into his life. Whether that means to you
that he would sing, or mourn, or be lessened.
And his patience when he rose up again
and took himself the long way
toward his kingdom, not knowing
if it had all changed, or if love
had lasted, or if anything can last.
Think of him as though he were your life,
as though you had sat waiting at a loom
for long, dark years, weaving and unweaving
what you are. Think of your life returning to you

with eyes that had seen death. And whether
you would look away if you saw him
pausing a moment among the gardens
and the horses, listening to the song
of each thing, the common things he had forgotten.
Think of him hearing your voice again,
hiding his face in his hands
as he listened, hearing a music
of losses and joys, pestilence
and bounty, a beauty that had prepared
a place for him. And whether you would have him
be changed by that, or return
to what he was, or become
what he had come this way to become.

Victoria C. Flanagan

Orchardist: Off-Duty

Kershaw, SC

I say give me a cigarette,
sipping chilled lager with a slack fist, thinking
of a man I knew from prison—that total upset,

off-set time of my life. He said
crime was a matter of opinion, his mind a burst
amid routine, before the old heaves

of the repeat offender. Each day, up at five.
Wipe thin gravy from the breakfast trays, whiff
yellow onion, butter sear, and the close-to-kitchen stitch

of his past to this, now. On the yard, chin-wag
with the boys about the best bleach for chef whites.
Lights out'll come real quick. I say yeah, when we met,

he was swallowed by the locked gate's fuss and croon,
had a boy's taste for mechanics—the tinker
in the tank, he joked. Fast fingers and no car, said

he couldn't keep away from a bottle or
an engine block. But in the prime of his confinement,
he touted the traps of his girl: *the* girl, his ol' girl,

that old maid, that one sweet woman remembered
in quick spins of nostalgia. See, I got plucked out
on a break when a major sting pushed capacity,

all those inbound lifers an answered prayer,
and he told me to breathe for him, to not
neglect the top notes: lemongrass, coriander,

orange peel. I say my greatest fear
is a lull that would press me into that loop.
Yeah—I fear the on-a-dare, through-the-window slip.

No such thing as second-round luck.
And most nights all I taste is smoke
and sweat and peaches.

Henryk Ross
204 | 554

The moisture of the earth turns the photographs to ghosts and white flames. Still, in one you can see a wagon of children led by a donkey going to an awful place. In another, a wagon returns, filled with loaves of breads that look like children, warm in the sun.

Samantha Grenrock

On Moving to Canada

When I was young I thought everyone in the world was American.
We all thought everyone was American,

or American in waiting, seeing America in the shapes of dust
kicked up behind a transport. The places they lived had no name

but America. Even what we bombed
stealthily, under the green of night vision, that was America at heart.

How do you leave America? Pursued
in a show of strength and conviction, blindfolded

for your own safety. Crossing the supposed crossing, hinterland that isn't,
is more of the same road. Towns twinkle far apart.

No crosshatched tendrils of concrete, familiar travails of travel.
Cars pass politely on the left. Vowels shift.

We are getting farther into the vastly forested, vastly uninhabited,
passing the rocky islet with the lone red fishing shed,

the rusted mountain where juniper berries bloom as petrified roses.
Baleen whales wash ashore and take three generations to become clean

bone, the vertebra hollow like a bird's, each larger than my pelvis.
The singular highway is at the mercy of wildlife, and no one drives after dusk.

Here, where we are taken by kind strangers, history is mostly uninteresting
stretches of land changing hands and abundant natural resources.

The first settlers must have looked around themselves, at a loss
for names of great men, and searched the landscape for epithet—

Yellow Knife, White Horse, Moose Jaw—or took the local word,
those difficult syllables with simple meanings. *Where the river narrows, beautiful waters.*

Samantha Grenrock

Capital One

Credit feels good in the mouth.
The root of the tongue draws glyphs from the throat,

frequencies thickened toward the tooth ridge.
Like the thing itself, unexpectedly stable,

a fetish is something more than. Or a rectangle,
matte black, heavier and more magnetic,

found floating near Saturn,
shaking awful sound out of the vacuum.

At given time t, a sliver of this or that dimension
is delayed getting here. Like light,

a wave sent back at great length
from the future or the distant past,

which are the same thing. In hand,
the coordinates are mesmerized, meant to be touched.

Benjamin S. Grossberg

Lucas Texts

The bell rings—
my phone is set to bells—
and it's you. You text

the commonplace. You text
your classes for the day.
What's due. You text

dinner: tuna fish. *Brain food.*
You text morning and say
It's morning!

You text night: *'night.*
You reference our
shared fetish—

a penchant for body hair.
Furred texts. Texts
that start or end

with "Grrr," which signifies
desire in a bear's growl.
Then you text the word "growl."

Pavlov's dogs salivate
for the bell. The plasticity
of dogs: breeding merely

for shapes—the curve
of ear, the pointed or rounded
snout—we can turn

wolf to poodle
in fifteen generations.
If I weren't so close to it

I'd say something
definitive about the plasticity
of men. The bell rings—

my mouth goes wet,
my abdomen, tight.

My Prom Dress

isn't ready yet, so I walk outside in my shorts and dark makeup, my Echo and the Bunnymen T-shirt to meet the limo my boyfriend and his best friend sprung for, my hair standing four inches overhead, while back in the kitchen, my mother sews frantically, because there's no minute like the very last minute. And the neighbors come out because: limo, tuxedos! On our cul-de-sac. On the cusp of a city before it crumbles into desert. It's 1987. One girl in a chiffon yellow gown dances with her date. The other girl, barefoot, toes a rock on the sidewalk, her nails the neon orange of the dress she awaits. And it seems like she's always waiting, longing for something to begin, before she rushes on to the next thing. And this is where I would join her again, step back into the body she doesn't know is as perfect as it will be. The world is not perfect, but it opens to her. I want to tell the girl: this is the moment. Look up! People are dancing in your driveway! Your mother summons you for one last measurement, and then, finally, the dress goes on, its puffy sleeves as big as your hair. You walk out to the sound of the neighbors' applause. Slow down, take it in. The driver is holding the limo door open, your boyfriend waiting; look at him, so crazy in love he almost can't stand it. Do a little twirl. Why not? Lift up the hem and flash them the shoes you dipped into a bowl of orange dye last night. Everything's the way you wanted it. What does it matter that you'll have to scrap the fancy dinner for a burger joint? Your mother's behind you, still holding her measuring tape. Turn around, give her a hug. No, it wouldn't be uncalled for to wave like a beauty queen, blow a few kisses before you duck into the long, black car.

Amanda Galvan Huynh

You Have To Be Ready

when they are—
my mother hands me
        dishes to wash—
even when you're not.
        I watch her turn

the faucet on,
        my hands heat
under the water
        and I wonder
who told her

        she had to be open
twenty-four/seven.
        How many times
did she lie, split
        open, reviewing

a mental list of things
        to be done tomorrow?
Did she learn
        over the years:
where to kiss,

        when to touch,
how to suck to help
        her husband finish
quick—to end
        the chore. To make

more time to be
              the good wife, the one
who makes floorboards
              reflect the moon
when it comes

              through the window,
to make sure
              he doesn't drift into
another woman's body—
              to say yes.

Bull's Eye

The truth is that wherever
an arrow lands, something like
a bull's eye opens.
—D. Bonta

Though you may count to 99,000 blossoms,
that number is but a sliver offered
to assuage the sorrows of this world.

The truth is a cascade of fragile blooms: they weave a ceiling
high above a forsaken sea. But the truth is also the bud;
its one jewel, bright like an eye, too soon taken away.

The truth is, the cab driver has no recourse but to say *Yes, please, No,*
officer, Yes, I understand as he bends his head beneath a barrage of abuse
while the customers in the back seat surreptitiously make a recording.

The truth is, the bull sees as well as he needs to and shits anywhere
he wants. In myths, the bull is a god and he rams himself into the girl.

This is what the bull does to remind himself he is a god.

The truth is, in the end, a whipping post; a shaming, an autopsy lesson.

Each instance, the moment or moments before some onlooker might have cried out,
Stop that. Or simply, *No.* Is the knife nicking the ear before it plunges into the wood.

Luisa A. Igloria

Hollowed

I like the sound of rice or bits of gravel falling through a cylinder of bamboo.
I like the way this dry rain falls in the vertical hollow of this space.

The rushing sound resembles water and is pleasing to the ear; it's possible
to slow the grains' descent with obstacles thrust at intervals within the tube.

On the bare arm, on the shoulder, on the back: the *mambabatok* taps with inked
needle and a mallet the figure for mountain, almost identical to water.

High above the Pacific, a hurricane whirls like a monstrous flower—
in its center is a cup where all the moisture in the world has thinned

to the sound of stacked bracelets. In the highlands where we lived,
the women fasten hawk bells to the ends of belts, and on their palms,

clap a devil-chaser. When they walk at dusk from the fields, the sound makes
a small nimbus— matter struck on matter, penetrating the spirit world.

Marlin M. Jenkins

Evolution

I was a boy and then
I switched from milk.

I was a moth and then
a boy plucked the wings

and rubbed them into
freshly-sprouting stubble.

I was a stumbling block
and then

the wood cracked
straight through

and from the outside
you couldn't see the splinters.

I was a monster
and now

I am a monster
still

just with different teeth.

I Should Have

I should have been mother-
fucking Black Mamba.
—Vernita Green, *Kill Bill*

I should have worn different shoes when I started running. I should
have seen each strand of spider web before they reached across my face,
wrapped around me like handwraps across knuckle and wrist. How long
can the wraps stay white before stained by sweat, if not blood?
What's in a white-lipped namaste? My love rose from a red
red rake. A boy closed the screen door on my head and left
a red stripe. It was not unintentional. Lucky it was only the screen door.
Lucky my face fell off and a titanic ant emerged, mouth first,
and carried the boy away like dead kin. He went where
everyone who left my neighborhood went. There went the neighborhood
when all the people of color left. I can understand bullshit
enough to write it—sometimes have trouble hearing it without subtitles.
Once, a practice session with a catalogue-bought wakizashi
left my own skin on metal tip and blood blotting out my eye. I should have been
subcutaneous. Should have been newly laid
concrete. In school, we couldn't speak
Arabic. As in, there was a rule. All the same for me
because I couldn't speak much anyway. All the same, they wanted us
all the same. All the same, I learned to fight from a woman
who had never fought herself, though she had fought herself.
We checked our bags after class for roaches amid the pads
and rubber knives. One of our first lessons was learning how to fall,
our small bodies on the hard-tiled floors in whichever church
we could convince to have us.

Marci Rae Johnson

3D Printed Meat:
It's What's for Dinner

How will we throw our blood against
the sides of the altar now? Red dye #5 is thin

and does not cling to stone, doesn't bake
in shades of rust & flame, in scarlet, folly,

vermillion & wine. Smoke is no longer necessary,
though fire should be kept burning continually.

Will the smell of plastic be a pleasing aroma
to the Lord? The singed hair and vinegar,

rotten eggs, faint apples forgotten
in their fields? The burning of rubber

and marigolds. Though the 4 corners
of the printer do not represent the edges

of the world nor the power of the Lord
to contain it, the fire shall not go out.

You will have a great beef dinner in no time at all.
No knives are needed. No son, beloved, to bind

upon the stone. It will cut like butter
from a can, the spray-on flavor no different

from the one you knew when you carved
the meat yourself, the flank and loin,

the tongue, the cheek to turn. Return. You know
which parts to wash and which to burn.

Hold him fast, little edible prototype, bloodless
sacrifice, broken for us.

Sarah Jordan

Fragment Memoir

1. you experienced the end at the beginning but since you didn't actually die: you're stuck, you are aware of the dominant narrative theory at hand and you don't have a choice. the dunes washed out with the rising water of the hurricane eroding your childhood. against a clothesline tentatively strung in the backyard you lined up flowers because you thought they would survive without soil beneath them. hook, line & seagull causing a ruckus on the pier where you cried *poor thing* and you didn't want the spectacle but you wanted the lure back. get a good look at the funnel rising: the smoke is unraveling threads. every morning repeating, *good morning brother*, studying the dominant narrative theory in terms clearly stating: keep your mouth shut. you don't have a choice & he keeps singing to you *i lv y s mch tht t hrts m hd*. you smell panic on subway cars. are you sure that's exactly what happened?

2. you are riding a backwards loop where the brick under your feet isn't on fire yet your soles are split in two. there's a shelf in your basement with a box of sex wax next to some old lionel trains and your house is like those bricks in that it is not on fire. your mother sitting on the porch drinking rolling rock (long stem bottle) repeating *four tons of rock these hands have laid their last wall*. what do you miss? the sound a telephone used to make as you violently hung up on a terrible conversation. with your mother. you are writing the best poetry when you are sleeping: it's the best because you can't remember. she says to you to find five five things that you see hear feel but you know, you know you think you know, grounding you in this room is a bad idea. retrospectively speaking: are you sure that's exactly what happened ma'am?

Vladislav Khodasevich
translated from the Russian by Ian Probstein

Rachel's Tears

Peace to this land nightly and sinful!
Pools, handrails and glasses sparkle.
I am slowly walking under the rain,
My shoulders are wet and my hat is soaked.
These days we have all become homeless,
As if we were wanderers ever,
And the rain is ceaselessly singing
About the ancient tears of Rachel.

Let descendants recite their legends
About their grandfathers with proud love —
Every day marks our hearts
With sin, tears and blood.
Woe to us whom God forced to come
Into this world in a fearful hour!
Along the cheeks of an old woman stream
Those bitter tears of Rachel.

I will defy glory and honor
If just a week ago she received
A stiff rug stained with blood
Of her only son's overcoat.
Oh, no matter how many songs
We sing bent under the heavy burden —
There is but the only refrain:
Inconsolable tears of Rachel.

1916

Patrick Kindig

getting swole: delts

look at your wings, brah: you're
a fucking bird. you're a starfish,

a seaturtle, vitruvian, brah,
the perfect size for the space

your body fills. & that space
is huge, brah, smells like sweat

& cinnamon. which is you,
the way you smell, & when

you raise your arms, it enters
me, brah, climbs down into

my lungs. & when i watch you, i can
feel it: those little pieces of you

in there, touching the soft
lining of my throat. i

can feel them moving, brah,
slithering their way down, feel

the way my body catches them
& changes their shape. turns

them into something else,
brah, turns them into blood.

Adie Smith Kleckner

Amelia Earhart Folds Origami Cranes

The fastest way to circumnavigate is to fold
the quiet black between stars.

Because I was unafraid to pull back the sky and look above,
the Earth unwinds a halftone map at my feet.

Gradations of light—porcelain white,
cowrie shell, bone china, mother of pearl—
are all just white against the unexplored other.

In pigment, white is the color of nothing.
Does the spiral end or just tighten imperceptibly?

Disappearance is dissonance, is to fall inside the folds,
is a riddle. The solution is folded in my pocket.

Loss is measured in degrees.
I fold the map into wings, the horizon is a crease

between ocean and sky. The radio is a
shell pressed to my ear.

Adie Smith Kleckner

Boy Without Wings

Kandahar, Afghanistan

The other boy—the insurgent who threw stones and insults and handmade
explosives the size of a dove, the boy with the anger of the trodden on—
he wanted the airiness of sand tossed into the wind.
His death was a multiplication of self, weapon of flesh.
Later we will find the contents of his pockets in the most unusual places.

When that other boy is gone, *this* boy steps forward.
Knowing nothing else, *this* boy still dreams of his lover. But something has silenced
the memory of the stuttering wing beats of her breast in his hand,
how the last yellow light slatted through the window, and as a child—only
really two or three years ago—he had fallen asleep watching the dust drift like fish
in the hot air. His mother on the other side of the door.

The moment before he steps forward, before he pulls or presses or ignites
the weapon—his just-still-warm, just-still-pulsing with blood and life, body—is the space
between call and echo. All gods grow silent in the waiting.

Virginia Konchan

Testimony

The day's preamble is this.
You are my hollow, my
absentee ballot, my lake.
Sorrow is my dry goods store.
Bedazzlement keeps us awake.
In the evening, I listen to the
lowing of cows. In the thick of it,
the blue-veined breast of it,
the moon does nothing but yield.
It's said grief is a private matter:
I say joy is the real lone wolf,
a Yellowstone park ranger
in khaki, answering to no one
but the sun and field.

Brandon Krieg

I Find Not Following

Web across my way
I find not following

bees into late
into gold opening:

tall-grass field
set far aside
lest in it we stop talking

and see into the ease
of all no-use

silver undersides of leaves
wind lifts

and be left
as barbed seeds

to wander not intending.

Kimberly Kruge

Live from the U.S.

Over a pirated connection you can get prime time.
Packets, switches, a deal between routers and the Tropicana commercial is your hostage.

Tonight you can hear. You can separate sounds. You can see the synth that plays a tinkling jingle
invoking the utmost security that only reduced-sugar OJ and prime time television can:

what with nuclear missile silos turned luxury shelters in Kansas—complete with red dental chairs,
a shooting range, and images of a goneworld lighting windows that look out onto the lithosphere.

Tonight you think this idea is the grave: goneworld. Say that three times fast. And where
do you end up in your mind? The Tropicana spokesmother switched out now for another,

one with a big backyard, a mosaic patio and a brood of beautiful children from every corner
of the world. And vitamins. You know what you have been known to say:

flowers on the table/a fissure in the family. Tonight, you can separate the spokesmother from
the children, from the lawn, from the dancing array of vitamins and the courtship of health.

Tonight, four-chord tunes don't move you to tears. A clip about better banking doesn't frenzy up
your mind as you x-out the possibility of To Have for To Have Not. But you'll be alright.

A striking fact about the luxury silos: a guard with a semiautomatic weapon keeps their watch.
A miraculous apocalypse survivor? One who doesn't mind not surviving? You know what

you have been known to feel: empathy for the gatekeeper. Special empathy for the doomed.
Extra special empathy for the wholly self-sacrificing. You know you aren't that good.

The prime time program runs its course. Boys and girls and girls and boys falling in love.
Talking about their future as if it were a smooth marble they warmed in their hands,

that they could toss out and collect again. Something finished and with limited purposes:
entertainment and diversion. Hearing them talk is almost enough. You could almost

forget what you know—more importantly, forget what you think—and gather someone you love
up in your arms and bore a hole into the mess of everything

(really, everything was the word you wanted there)
and linger a little before the virtual window, unhindered.

Rosa Lane

Black-Eyed Susan

Coned eye juts your fanned hip, crowns
a cincture of rays laid back: mustard

symbol of fair play, caution signal, or the Ojibwa's
poultice packed on a snake bite. You, child

of the sunflower, poor-land daisy, golden
Jerusalem, English bull's-eye, black-eyed Susan

& it's Susan I want to talk to. I want
to tell her how easily the wind lifts

her golden pleats, ray by ray, how I see
her thigh, coarse trichome hairs, the one

green leg run *the long meadow* towards light,
her last openness before sunset. Now

in our bedroom, you drop your skirt,
a touch of sun still lingers there. You cinch

evening at your waist, slip into a slip
I hike. Each radius pulled back to the inner ring,

& all your cultivars I have learned
to commemorate even in Baltimore when horses

Run for the Black-eyed Susans & a circlet
of black eyes is placed on the winning neck.

& when it's Indian summer, rays deepest
marmalade, I go & go for your double gold.

Crying It Out

"Psychologist: Crying It Out
Damages Baby's Brain,"
Parenting Magazine

Blood can't curdle. It turns silver, a stream
of mercury so cold I can wash a dish.

Tra la. The kid cries. Each wipe of the sponge
is a vowel in the treatise against me.

You're burning down cities
of children, inner mothers murmur. *Your purgatory*

is washing the same plate. I whistle and
the child screams and the dish pile shrinks.

Her cry is a chord tied
to an organ I inhaled at her birth

called the End of Autonomy.
When she stops, my body hums like a field.

Some women blend bits
of their placenta into their smoothies.

It helps with depression, they say, to eat
a piece of what sustained the baby,

to take it back. To say, *Darling,*
this was mine all along.

Brenna Lemieux

Apology

Forgive me, my love, for the little joke: *if we're still together,*
I said, inviting you to the year-out wedding whose save-the-date

I'd just unwrapped. I am used to losing my best things,
the gold thread earrings I splurged on, the apartment I gave up

to move in with my ex. My other ex, the fragile *peace* we built
from clean dishes and wide berths. I use *peace* instead of *love*.

I use *we* instead of *I*. Frankness that veers into hope in the habit
of someone who learned to gloss the versions she told her parents.

Bear with me. What I mean is: stay. What I mean is, I can't
imagine a reason to truss myself in the gauze claws of pantyhose

if you won't be there when I peel them off. When I started,
I was cautious. It mattered to be right. But the end of love

does not make it less real. We are in the throes of each other,
we are in thrall. If we are still together next year, I will thank

the stars, the saints, the dozing fates who intertwined our lives
and haven't snipped the thread. I will offer my clumsy secular praise:

an off-key song, outstretched arms. The eighth-note footfalls
of my morning run, a quiet consecration of the street,

of my lucky thrumming skeleton: yes, and yes, and yes.

Maja Lukic

The Revolution

Spice rack and a foot caught in crossfire

Eyetooth and a blueberry soaking in acid

A blonde wig and nerves preserved in salt

Serpent slips past a blockade at a riot

The dancer eats a mushroom in the academy

Dead child in the honeypot, inner tissues blackening

The autopsy will turn up a piece of chalk and a sprig of mint

The autopsy will turn up an arm and a clam lolling in the cradle

The dictator has sex with a capsicum during the siege

Noise everywhere and schoolbooks on the tanks

Propaganda bombs the buffet table

For days, we pick up fragments of marzipan and meringue

A carcass as a wartime puppet

We make it dance at the wedding reception

Angie Macri

Became an
ark, carved

from the mountain, launched
into a new sea. A year slid
down a girl's face watching
for a shore. Became
all the cities
under the keel, skyscrapers
still pointing, the trees
as sawyers marking
the old earth.
Fall formed a nocturne
of drowning, the sun
above like god
saying nothing, white bending.
The girl was carved
from skyscrapers, the top
of her head a city garden,
and the sea grew tenderly,
the sun above, a point,
a keel burning.

Jennifer Manthey

To Become A Man

I board a boat and wave goodbye
to my mother.

In the beginning of the 19th century, men's fashion emphasized broad shoulders with puffs at the sleevehead.

I lean into the rail, push through my flesh
until I feel bone.

Many men wore whalebone stiffened waistcoats with lacing at the back.

There, I think, is my hardness.
I knew it was there.

Tails of the coat were narrow, pointed, and fell just below the knee.

A man must be ready to duel —
I would cut a bullet from my own thigh.

Shirts of linen or cotton featured tall standing collars and were worn with wide cravats tied in a soft bow.

Like any woman in labor,
a surgeon breathes

Trousers were cut full through the hips and thighs, tapering to the ankles.

in and out.

A man's shoes were narrow, heelless slippers with low-cut vamps.

I was first to believe it —
a child could be cut from his mother
and the mother could live.

Waistcoats were buttoned high on the chest.

When I die I suppose you will unwrap
my body against my wishes,

Pants featured a small waistline and flared out slightly at the hip with small pleats, creating the image of fullness in the hip region.

see the story of birth
I keep hidden on my stomach.

Double-breasted coats were very much in fashion.

The first British doctor to perform a cesarean section where both mother and baby lived was Dr James Barry, who, it was discovered after his death, was actually a woman named Margaret Bulkey. She disguised herself as a man for 56 years in order to study at medical school and practice medicine in the British Army.

Maya Marshall

Girl Secrets in
Her Own Cocoon

To have a door! The back of which she could
wake to, smile at, brush her girl lips and hips
against. At night, she'd sit cross-legged
on the floor, press her knees to the door's face.
In her room, she'd deny her mother
entry, adorn herself in costume jewels
and pick her hair out round. She'd say yes
to her own face, neither too dark or too much her
daddy's. In her mirror, she'd perfect her
smile—with teeth, without—smack her lips,
play woman without her mother's boyfriend
telling her *feed me a little a this*
fish. She'd take her cue from Martha Reeves,
jerk and gyrate. She wouldn't need *nowhere to run*.

Petar Matović
translated from the Serbian by Vesna Stamenković

On the Razor's Edge

This year the lindens are late blooming.
Once again, Ana won't come back from Greece,
and I've painted my room yellow: it's soothing.

Each morning I wake up tired and sweaty,
the moment before lighting that first cigarette
is an idea of matches, rhythm, and verse.

I haven't a wholeness. My insides are a cormorant
with a scarf around its neck. When I wander,
I don't feel like Odysseus, or Ahasuerus either.

Each time, examining the razor's blade with my thumb
before shaving, I promise that I'll write a poem,
as soon as I'm happy with myself.

Iulia Militaru
translated from the Romanian by Claudia Serea

Nomad Linguistics

the language compels;

       there is an imposed/need of knowing

    the meaning of the words,

when you want to tell

    something to the other.

The Ministry of Internal Affairs will be able to mandate, through executive decision, the removal from the urban agglomerations of any individuals who can't justify their presence in those areas, as well as the removal from any town of those who, through their acts against the working people, damage the building of socialism in the People's Republic of Romania. Those said individuals will be ordered to a forced domicile in any other settlement.

1. 'I'm leaving' is the title of a novel.
2. You never destroyed the objects, just left.
3. We had to keep our gate closed at all times.

Ling-uistics = *a scientific study, heterogeneous and multi-shaped, as its specific research subject is the language, the tongue, or the speech.*

"Nomad." It is known that the language, in order to be communicable, has to go through a long search. A road. That meaning attaches itself, by force, or by chance, to the circulating words.

No/mad = a person or a group that doesn't have a stable settlement, that moves from place to place, that wanders. Each dictionary acts like a closed gate.

1. In return, no one tells us anything.
2. About the journey of some children.
3. On a train. Then, on an infinite/field.

All our fun consisted in playing on those vast plains. In summer, we took the cattle to the fields, to-gether with other children our age. When it comes to playing, the kids' resourcefulness is infinite. We found new ways to play without toys.

Comparisons are always useful for building a (high)way. In an open space, as far as the eye can see. That's how a comm-unity is born. I am just a comm-unist who deports your speeches. In a space hostile to communication. Forcing them to communicate, to live there.

The people, including pregnant women, the old, the sick, and small children, were put on cattle train cars and taken to the Bărăgan Plain. After the train ride that took two weeks, they got off in the open Bărăgan field, far away from any human settlement, and they were ordered to build their own houses. The land has been divided into lots with the plow, and each lot had a stake holding a sign with the house number. Thus, in the summer and fall of 1951, in the Ialomita and Galati regions, 18 new villages were built, and they were:

Brateş, Bumbăcari, Dâlga, Dropia, Ezerul, Fundata, Lăteşti, Măzăreni, Movila Gâldăului, Olaru, Pelican, Răchitoasa, Rubla, Salcâmi, Schei, Valea Viilor, Viişoara, and Zagna

1. An instinct of movement was left in us.
2. From a meaning to another, in/a chain.
3. Searching for an inaccessible reader. Searching for…

We are told that language can do more, it wants more, more than the simple communication of information through ideas. Without reality.

We were working in the collective garden and in the cotton field. They took us out of school and gave each one of us a purse that seemed huge (as I was little) and I carried it with me. But that purse didn't fill up! My hands were raw from picking. That's how they got us, from school, marching in a column, they gave us bags and we were ordered to pick, in rows. At the end of the day, we had to bring back the bags, full.

Since then,

an instinct of movement was left in us. Re-
run.

1. I am not a linguist, nor a philosopher, nor a… I'm not etc.
2. "I" am limiting myself to the forced association of speech fragments that escape.
3. They are involved in their own deportation.
4. They are removed even more, swarm the surface, go through definitions, then return to the first context.
5. In vain. Something else is there.

My nephew, my sister's kid, was three months old when he was deported. There was also a newborn baby… Greta Dontu was born on June 16, and, on June 18 at night, she was taken—only three days old—only to be thrown on that field. The children were swarmed by ants, by flies, such was their life. If the silence and stillness of the animals is superior to ours, then we have to stop at our words. We have to communicate to be inferior to animals, to be humble.

1. Only humility and movement can stop us.
2. Etc.

Translator's Note:
The poem is built using fragments of official language used by the government of communist Romania in contrast with the language used by victims of deportations from the Western part of Romania to the Eastern, scarcely populated Bărăgan Plain between 1951 and 1956. In this interval, over 40,000 people were deported. 1,700 died, of which 174 were children. The poem explores the movement of language in relationship with the movement of people and history.

Pamela Miller

My Husband the Science Fiction Writer Tells Me About His Childhood

—for Richard

I grew up facedown
in Chicago's spongy suburbs.
We ate dinner every night at the Heap O' Beef
and bought clothes at the House of Sad Plaid.
We vacationed down turnpikes bland as envelopes,
mailing ourselves off to some dank lake.

My mother switched on her minuscule TV
and watched nothing, nothing, nothing
for sixty years.

My dad was so cheap
he signed his name in blood,
too skinflint to invest in a pen.

My behemoth of a brother
"managed" my allowance,
snapping nickels in half and giving me neither.

So I hunkered in the attic like Quasimodo,
my defiant hair down to my knees,
reading *Famous Monsters of Filmland* magazine
and *The Tinfoil Hat Review*,
waiting for my rocket legs to sprout
and blast me into breathable air,
for my mind to stretch wide as a hovering spaceship
beaming me up to myself.

Nicole Miyashiro

Unsung

—for the Unsung Founders
Memorial (UNC Chapel Hill),
2005 (black granite, bronze
sculpture) by Do-Ho Suh

This is not a surrender. Arms raised. Bodies clustered, cast together. This is bronze. Fingers pressed to a slab. This is a table. A whole people beneath. This is where giants use boulders as stools, stones like the unmarked graves of slaves that have rolled. And been rolled away. Here is the table's surface. A black mirror in the rain. A place for conversation. A place for meals. For a book, splayed and pored over. This is a table. A weight. Of withheld cakes. Of coveted wines. Flexed elbows of giants, needling their own furniture. Here is where they put their feet up. Against the pedestal of bodies. See here how knees shine. Noses shine. The women, their breasts shine. Because they are bronze. Between soil and slab. Hands weight-bearing the feast, the sated appetites. Dripping candles and burn of wax. Here is where giants rest their feet. Tread soles against human parts. See how the bodies shine. In marked places. The people. Made of bronze. No single one identified. Not a single one standing alone. This is not a surrender.

Faisal Mohyuddin

Whenever He Teaches *Hamlet*

He forgets the tune to his baby boy's favorite
lullaby. He forgets to fasten his seatbelt before
    driving away. He forgets to dog-ear the spot
where he gave up on another self-help book.
    He forgets that stillness does not mean you stop

breathing. He forgets to put the leftovers in
    the fridge, to soak the pots and pans. He forgets
to feed his family of pet goldfish, forgets to say
    their names before leaving for work. He forgets
that Hamlet once had a father, too. He forgets

    which way is Mecca. He forgets his best friend's
name, forgets to ask about his dying cat, about
    his dying tomatoes. He forgets he doesn't believe
in ghosts. He forgets to shampoo his hair, forgets
    he no longer has any hair. He forgets to pick up

the dry-cleaning, forgets to finish buttoning
    his shirt. He forgets to eat breakfast, forgets to
pack a lunch. He forgets to call his mother
    on her birthday. He forgets the anniversary of
his father's death. He forgets his phone at work,

    forgets to check his mailbox before leaving school.
He forgets to like a former professor's post about
    his newly published book of poems. He forgets
the man is slowly going blind. He forgets to pray
    the morning prayer until after the sun has risen.

He forgets to tell his students Hamlet is really not
        crazy, that his paralysis is all about the pain of
a broken heart, of a grief that endures. He forgets
        to mail the check to the electric company, forgets
to set up automatic bill pay, forgets to inquire

        if they might waive the late fee, again. He forgets
nobody is supposed to remember everything.
        He forgets to take his vitamins. He forgets the Urdu
word for loneliness, forgets the Punjabi word for
        loneliness, forgets the English word for loneliness.

He forgets to post the homework assignment for
        his first period class, forgets to check work email
once he gets home, forgets Hamlet really isn't crazy,
        forgets not to blame him for being so heartbroken.
He forgets to brush his teeth before going to bed.

        He forgets to take out the bathroom trash, forgets
what it means to let go, to move on, to let memory
        bring comfort, not agony. He forgets it hurts
others when he forgets, forgets it hurts him
        when he hurts others with forgetting. He forgets

the password to his online banking account, forgets
        the cat has been dead for a long time, that those
tomatoes survived, and were quite sweet. He forgets
        his father in his final weeks asked him to clean his
childhood bedroom, to remove all his old books,

forgets he's still not finished the job. He forgets to
tie his shoes, to zip his fly. He forgets how old he is.
      He forgets those are birds trilling in the tree outside
his window, not noisy angels on vacation. He forgets
      to wash the paper cut on his finger before putting

on a Band-Aid. He forgets to cry at the funeral,
      forgets to bring flowers, forgets to tell his mother
he is sorry. He forgets to tell his wife he is sorry.
      He forgets to tell his son, his students—the rest of
the world—he is sorry. He forgets the significance

      of Ramadan, forgets to wait for the sun to set
before breaking his fast with two dates and a glass
      of water, forgets to spit out the pits. He forgets to
show up for jury duty, forgets to reschedule, forgets
      if it's even possible to reschedule. He forgets he does

actually believe in ghosts, in giving them a chance
      to explain themselves. He forgets to buy diapers,
wipes, the right brand of fancy organic unsweetened
      almond milk from that new fresh market next to
the abandoned currency exchange. He forgets

      to get gas. Again, he forgets about poor Hamlet,
forgets a broken heart can undo even the most normal
      person's grip on things. He forgets that inside his heart,
where he thinks there is nothing, there sits a room
      in which he can lock himself on days when he doesn't

know where else to go. He forgets he still remembers
      the words to the lullaby, that his son is old enough
now to help him remember the tune, to hold him
      together until the final scene when most everyone
dies and the living can finally go back home.

Cheswayo Mphanza

Dap

Our fingers dive, cross and hook,
sewing crooked alphabets mid air.

Chicago's morning rust hidden
between our ridges. The heat

we steal from something
or someone warmer than us

to soothe the ash around
our hands. Our palmar sides

wrapping each other's fingers.
Tracing the scabs, callouses,

and craters in our knuckles.
How we test our strength

and memory of what lethal language
these hands have inherited. How we lock

and hold, waiting for the other
not to let go. Our offering is a language

of bruised tendons and ligaments. A prayer
we scribe through sky. Brother, I long

for your palms to graze mine,
pulling me closer into the vacancy

of your chest and easing my back
　　　when you hold me, knowing

　　　I am kept by the malice you reserve
for those who don't share our embrace.

Elisabeth Murawski

Intentions

Coils of belting
snake in the rear of the truck
reeking of leather
and smoke, whiskey
and Smith Brothers cough drops.

She sees him coming from the flat,
slides the bottle back
under the seat
where she found it, slips out,
spy with proof

who'll never tell.
Sipping Kool-Aid
as she rocks on the porch,
she thinks of good intentions
easily botched: the iron

too hot on satin, the best
China plate slippery as soap.
Wonders if he's cursed
as she is,
if he, too, means well.

She'll grow up
expecting from lovers
bouquets of yellow roses
like those he brings her mother
after a fight.

She'll grow up
thirsting, attuned to
his fear of drought, caught
between wanting him dead,
or alive forever.

Room 420

She stared
out the open
window.

Why can't
I be that
magnolia tree?

she said
and wept
into my hair.

Abby E. Murray

Asking for a Friend

Is there a way to tell
the commander's wife
you're a pacifist
and it's possible
to trust your spouse
but mourn his work
because the death
he's delivered
through the cracks
of thatched rooftops
is more than a fracture
beneath his skin
and the flag is a reminder
and gravel is a reminder
and pins and ribbons
and coins and the smell
of diesel and buildings
without doors are a reminder
and you won't secure
the gold battalion crest
over your left breast
no matter how many
times she tells you
it's like a sweetheart pin
and the last thing
you want when
your father is found
dead in his duplex
is an email asking when
she can drop off some
meatballs in sauce
and you can't stop

swaddling your brain
in yesterday's Times
to see what city has fallen
as if they topple
rather than burn
and you refuse to stop
reading and doubting
until no one makes sense
and every deployment
is a Talking Heads song
and every morning
is an invitation to dance
in a pill bottle
and you're not interested
in keeping busy
and you don't want
more group texts
and you don't want
your daughter learning
to shoot a rifle
with the other kids
who aim at a silhouette
of someone's son
tied to a haystack
and you don't want
to host a dress swap
before the gala
and you don't want
a souvenir photo
with the bald eagle
and every time
the commander says

let's thank our ladies
you want to toss the table
champagne flutes and all
and watch all the favors
you've done to prompt
his gratitude go flying
because you've tried to say
war is necessary
but the words are like
spiders in the shower
they have every right
to be there and yet
you are crawling up
the side of yourself
trying to get clean
without howling
and you don't want
to call them *our boys*
and you don't want
to be called *household 6*
or a rock or a pillar
and the only commanders
you trust are the ones
who seem pained
by the movement
of their own bones
given to them
by their mothers
freely and without
any mental reservation
and it's against your beliefs
to say things are fine
when the satellites
click and blink above us
unwilling to share
which target needs water
and which needs bread
and if anyone knows
a way to say this

without provoking
the commander's wife
to roll a wide stone
over your spouse
and his career
let's meet soon
I'll buy you a beer

Abby E. Murray

Time Capsule for My Daughter

You are three. It's the Year of Standing on Chairs
in the American Express Lounge at McCarran Airport,
announcing *the president does not like women.*
Already, two suits in the room are nodding in agreement with you.
Enjoy this. Their sons are thousands of miles away
waiting to touch your wrist and say *let me stop you there.*
You loathe the feel of shoes on your feet,
white laces tight across the tongue.
You would recognize Elizabeth Warren
if she bought groceries at our Safeway.
You fear the burn of silence delivered but shush your Lego people
under the kitchen table for hours, power in your mouth like caramel.
You know the difference between dissent and doghouse.
You know Snoopy deserves to defeat the Red Baron
but Manfred von Richthofen, when I say the name to you,
is the long O sound of facelessness.
Some stories you learn from me, some you pilfer from the radio.
This year, you ask about September 11 and I tell you
very bad men flew planes into buildings, killing people,
and it's a neighbor, not me, who tells you the city was filled with heroes.
My heart is sheathed like a Stanley knife no stethoscope can hear.
You believe children are too young to die because in all ways, this is true.
You know your dad is gone for long ribbons of time
but haven't put together what he might be doing:
the WWII half-track outside his office,
the bloody men on his book covers,
the flag in our garage still grey with skin cells and Afghan dust.
There are two world maps in our house
and you can point to Iraq but no one's told you
how small we are, that the head of a pin could crush us,
and in the context of these maps, no naked eye can see us.

Already, you accept language as permanence.
Already, you turn like a planet, pulling me
through each night on a wave of outrageous hope.

Amanda Newell

Butchering the Sika Deer

Bound by her hind legs,
she dangles from the maple—
so small she twirls a little
in the breeze. I watch him
as he works the knife slowly
along the split seam of the cow's
belly, peeling away the cotton
flaps of her hide like a sock
until nothing is left but flesh
wrapped in white swirls
of gauzy tissue. I did not teach him
how to call for his prey
on the marsh, how to shoot
a living thing, how to butcher it.
That was his father.
Like his father, he does not mind
the blood. He'll take what he needs,
nothing more. When he's done,
he'll drag what's left
of her into the woods.

Elizabeth O'Brien

Half Truths

an omission is a kind of lie,
my mother would say
as if forthrightness was a kind of virtue
as if it might be

some days are just easier
to make friends,
to lie

on this coat, thinking of the flowers
I guess
they may be
pansies, peonies, perhaps
I only prefer this
one word over the other, and she
frets at the buttons, a
rather cheap plastic, not bone,
or shell
or wood
might be perfect, indignant

and

it's a reminder of something

Ashbery might say, or
about the flowered coat I wear
only on certain days
to ally myself with Autumn,
because trench implies
not just dirty mouths
or ruts in the dust with men
in them,
but also slices of cake,
bright flowers;

she would sigh, *it's so lovely otherwise*, or
perhaps
fixation is not unlike fixing, or
a preoccupation
implying a kind of truth
one could say,
but I can't help myself

she seems so glad *finally* I've chosen
to wear something pretty

Alison A. Ogunmokun

Amtrak Stock/
Remnant Cognitions

Really lush before fall, the streams are murky and laden with ass stench.
I wonder about all my almost-boyfriends. They're missing out on me, maybe.

A trip from urban to rural is 'artisanal cookies' to 'I don't trust my neighbors not to shoot me.'
Late dinner might get you sexed, lunch crumbs follow you all day, and breakfast is a soft gaze.

A family passes by with lime corked and train shaken Coronas.
Birth control is snack banter.

An old woman sits alone, sips Moscato from a lipstick-smooched paper cup across the aisle.
All my almost-boyfriends live abroad. We broke up after I made them brunch.

This upholstery has been here since second wave feminism.
I'm the clunkiest black girl I know, I'll never make a man brunch again.

The sun is setting and I realize the whole train car will die someday.
Brunch stands naked and asks you to look. Brunch is considerate and seasoned to your taste.

I'm too poor for Amtrak wine so I opt for a blueberry muffin. It is the texture of mattress foam.
Brunch is not afraid of long distance. Brunch drives you to the airport, mourns your departure.

Crying baby, man foot tapping on one and three to reggae, couple in love, empty seat, lonely teen,
businesswoman, recently brunched young man, empty seat, empty seat, empty seat.

Paul Otremba

Midden

It could be worn stone, where water or wind
had visited, leaving behind scalloped bowls.
Perhaps the upturned curve of scapula
or cracked pelvis. Vast quantities of oysters,
a cheap and common food, were consumed
at the settlements. Could mean years.
Could mean hordes. The ice formed, then weakened.
He had gone past the point on the horizon,
then crossed back. It was a thin layer that year.
Roman tiles, an iron disk, fragments
of charred bone. She walked along the shore
collecting oyster shells, the hardened lips
of what had been loosened of their songs.
Which side meant sky? Which meant sea?
Perhaps it was a trade, a bargain not fully realized,
like the arrowhead accepted by the flesh.
Hands bound because the gods love talking
but not talking back. In the metaphor, the body
digs a cellar, stocks provisions for a siege
or hard winter. Then the waters opened
and took the ship whole. The waiter spoke
like you would to an accomplice—
what you're tasting is the sea.

Houndstooth
& Sparrow

I know that beauty has a price.
Like the sirens, it lures us from refuge
into a love that surpasses its pattern.

This is what Alexander McQueen
must have thought when he enlarged
houndstooth to avian proportions,

predicting his death by giving
bite-marks, wings. Once wounded,
every gesture holds a knife.

You can walk the runway.
Stare into its dark & watch
as strange wounds become sparrows,

but do not forget me.
Do not forget that morning in North Carolina
when Sawmill Creek appeared opalescent.

It too sun-struck.
Do not forget the muddy banks where
pine leaves became needle beds in the night.

Your body has a secret
and it is there I return in dreams:
the scarred rib, the drowned bird's call.

Doug Ramspeck

Mud Boys

Our sons today are throwing stones into the river.
And although the willow leaves rustling above them
are a kind of lexical quickness, I am focusing, instead,
on each new splash, am studying a hawk high above
the trees, am wondering about the slow thermals
of the years. Sometimes, of course, we are bereft inside
our ribs, the charred hours of a life becoming woodsmoke,
but today there seems a certain holiness in the manure
of my wife's garden, in her gripping of the trowel. Is this
how the living reconnoiter? And maybe there are prayers
for mud and prayers for an alluvial sky. Earlier, I know,
our boys were studying a discarded snakeskin curling
as a reliquary near the river's bank, but now their arms
are flinging out and out. And soon, I know, the dark blood
of dusk will be a lamentation, and later, perhaps, I will
lie awake and listen to the commotion of a freight train
rumbling in the distance, will imagine that carrion flies
are feeding on the skin of the moon. Or I will think of
my father in his final years, of his dandelion ghost head.
Didn't he know he was already gone, had given himself over?
Then maybe I will I dream of the years floating in their jar
of formalin, the decades like the catfish along the river
bottom, reaching and reaching with their barbels. But for
now—*now*—I will appreciate this rhythm of the rocks
dropping into the mud current, will watch the hawk pressing
the prow of its boat into a dimming summer sky.

Francisco Layna Ranz
translated from the Spanish by JP Allen

A Few Days Back, Somebody

A few days back, somebody
dictated a poem to me.
It was about first things
and I copied, faithful to his mandate.
I stopped, however,
a few lines in,
thinking about the effect
of interruption.
I can barely speak
of what came next.
He was talking as if near
was the same as far.
I stopped copying
when I saw the first silhouette.
I was afraid
my mother would appear
in his words.
It's gotten late
and it's starting to snow
—I said—
maybe some
other time.

Opening Lines

You keep asking where
I.m from.
I.ve said NYC twice /
twice.
Second generation.

You keep examining like /
like I.m
right now inventing
antebellum.

Like later, you won't try
to impress,
with a Wu-Tang lyric,
liberties with a
Chappelle set.

Like you don't know
where we are /
what we built.
Like you don't know
me.

You keep asking where
we.re from.
Like the hyphen sits with
no direction /
like we are still
in   between:

You keep
repeating
the question.

Merlin Ural Rivera

The Lonelies of Saint Petersburg

Saint Petersburg in March, a city beset with sighs, storm-tortured, dark.
My mother had brought the wrong shoes and she was mad at the guide
whose mother was dying and he left her alone with my father, who
thought the carriage ride was superfluous and dirty and he sat under
the blanket with his arms crossed as the horses pulled the black box
and got whipped by the driver who kept sighing as if he knew he was
the undertaker of this bond. I knew her when she was simply Leningrad,
my father bragged, as if the city was an actress who changed her worn-out name.

Women with furs around their necks studded the frost-minted streets,
and under a parade of transparent clouds, my mother and my father
wended their way, unguided. He, like a merchant who assessed
the value of each goddamn palace and cathedral. She, annoyed by his scoffs,
his heavy leather coat and those ugly, ugly pants under which she could see
the white socks she was expected to wash that night in that sickly hotel,
far from the river that spilled between the thighs of the city he loved as
a student, back when it was called Leningrad, and he, the math prodigy,
was sleeping with the ballerinas, as he called them—always in plural.
He wanted to look around—alone, if possible, walk by his old dorm,
see if Kalinka Café kept its velvet divans, and maybe, just maybe
Pavel would be there, waiting for him with a box of dominos and some beer.

But my mother wanted cheap jewelry and magnets from Nevsky,
and she called Kalinka a shithole. They ate pâté sandwiches in a wilted park
and waited for the city to say something. My mother's lips were bare as she
posed and posed for photos, as she forced a smile against the onion domes
of carnival-colored churches and explosive fountains. She cringed
when my father left swirly orange peels by the Blue Bridge
and he laughed at her when she bought the bust of Lenin
made of pure milk chocolate, and said let's eat his ears first.
He said my mother's name the way he always said it,
like a stranger soothing a lost child on a street corner.

On their last day, Smolny Cathedral rising like a wedding cake,
the Hermitage with its long horizonless rooms full of knights and Rembrandts,
and right in-between a swamp-like fight about who-knows-what.
They parted ways in the museum, and my mother frowned away in
the Majolica room under the ivory light seeping through a waterfall of curtains.
She cursed my father until she forgot about him and she never knew
that he sat in the cafeteria for hours, all by himself,
renouncing beauty and eating hard Russian candy.
Wrappers thrown on the sticky table like swirls of paint,
and a black notebook spread across his knees,
with pages full of numbers, stern and neat.

Lucid

We moved in the same circles, civil
like right-hand turns, singing hymns
of distraction up and down all those slow

pine highways between Harrison,
Stone, Perry, Jasper, Jones, Newton
counties. Something about the axle of his

hips, I liked about him. He had gone to college,
Alcorn. Once, he even came to Gulfport to see
me. Ahem. Don't give me that look, I know

what I'm saying, but you're underestimating
how vicious and narrow I kept my hemlines,
I knew how to sashay across a room

at precisely the right pace to leave a wake
of men in reverie. Back then, Medgar knew
the markers of a race woman when he saw one.

Hoax

Sherri Papini was found alive on Thanksgiving Day, 2016. Sherri Papini was covered in purple & blue clouds she called bruises. Sherri Papini's long hair was cut because her abductors had an aversion to blondes. Sherri Papini insists they were two Latinas. Had that vague but familiar outline of otherness—accents nasal, sentences quick with vowels falling from a cliff: ah, eh, ee, oh, oo. One of the women had curly hair, thin eyebrows, & pierced ears. Sherri Papini described the other woman, who was older, as having thick eyebrows with straight salt-and-pepper hair. Sherri Papini is not Tera Smith who has been missing since 1998. Sherri Papini is not a supermom. Sherri Papini is exactly what my cousin Carrie wished she looked like, especially after my grandmother told her to stay out of the sun: You prieta. I want to say "Sherri Papini" over & over again until I reach semantic satiation, emptying out all the marrow of meaning from her name. Sherri Papini insists her abductors did this with the word "flores"—one of the only words she remembered from high school. Her teacher made them all choose a name in Spanish. Hers was Margarita, for the daisy, not the drink. Now when she sees gumplant & poppy, she feels nothing, not even the scissors against her hair like a field of wheat.

Eric Roy

The Naked Bootleg
and the American
Distance

Scouting trips get me out of school early,
taking me to Plano, College Station, Navasota.
Off back roads and two lane highways
hide shacks where subtle smoke
bathes briskets, ribs, hot-guts sausage—
a holy trinity good as any other.
A beer or two. A game of pool or horseshoes.
Any game before the game where I have to fight back sleep.
Down and distance, formation, play action
called out in one long take, like a bedtime story.
Naked bootleg. End around. Crazy option.
Coach next to me driving the truck
on our way to War Memorial stadium
jokes about killing anyone who isn't white.
I tell him his blatant racism is refreshing
but the fact our team's half black is something I avoid.
People color the stands cheering for their children.
Afterward they talk about the game in terms of team.
My life five years from now: always passing
when I should have been establishing the run.
Spiking a wax cup of ambition in a dim blue Port-a-Can.
My son or daughter born and old enough
to ask, What happens when I die?
By the time I get home the moon's submerged in ice
but my wife is still awake and wants
mustard potato salad in a Styrofoam container
I'm holding tightly with both hands.

Austin Sanchez-Moran

Being Caught in
a Failing State

I wake up in a Holiday Inn in a former Soviet Bloc nation. I walk down the stairs to the lobby where there are men with guns saying they are members of the "Green Revolution." One knocks me out with the butt of his rifle.

I wake up in a cell that looks like the small chamber room of a medieval castle. I am still wearing pajamas. There are a couple other men that have just woken up dirty and confused. Before any conversation, a soldier opens the door and throws gardening equipment at us. "Work! Go!" We walk out and down a long, dark hallway to fields where others in pajamas are harvesting plants and others are hoeing the parched ground. Another soldier points and says, "That is tomato basil leaf crossbred and that is cactus aloe crossbred. You two over there, you, over here. Work."

I wake up the next morning and the cell's wall has crumbled and we all walk out of the hole where the window had been. We run towards the small city in the distance arriving to a crowd watching a large military parade and on one side of the main square a barricaded corner has a banner labeled, "Tourists." I run through the crowds sneaking up to two Brits in safari garb taking photographs. I open my mouth to ask, "Is this a coup?" but a lemon rind is suctioned to my teeth. The male tourist says, "I think this one needs help." And then the woman counters, "He's dirty though…" I'm screaming to say anything now. "Not a talkative fellow I see… Let's leave him." Tanks enter the square.

Hilary Sideris

Il Potere dell'Empatia

I'm learning to hear & see
without judging, reading
self-help in Italian, *osservare*

senza valutare. Thunderstorms
roll over Brooklyn, small
craft advisories, Amber alerts

rattle our phones. According
to philosopher J. Krishnamurti,
la forma piu' elevata di

intelligenza is empathy,
so I don't comment on your
stuck-to-fridge to-do list,

the many tasks so far
undone, the few crossed
off with black Sharpie.

Volker Sielaff
translated from the German by Mark Terrill

The Beauty of the Forest of my Childhood

Early in the morning I lay and dreamed
of chic chrome-gleaming bicycles:
handlebars frames wheels and country roads
with the asphalt sizzling in the sun
and burning fruit trees—yes burning fruit trees!
The summer detachment pulled on its uniforms
we'd heard that in the woods was a barracks for the "Volksarmee."
Some imagined SS-20s beneath the mushrooms and ferns
and once my brother—while picking mushrooms—
was arrested: they thought he wanted to steal their
rockets and then shoot them off from in front of
the local ice cream parlor.
As youths we parked our bikes against a tree
or left them to lie in the street
in the moonlight. Sat down next to them, puffed.
A girl from the village disco
floated as an angel above our heads and away
a sort of proclamation
only we didn't know for what.

Sarah Dickenson Snyder

Everyone Who Slept With Me in 1960

A rabbit named Bucky
with blue ears and dangly legs,

two trolls, one with orange
hair I called Fiery & one

with green called Tree,
a monkey named Zippy,

and PT (Princeton Tiger),
my favorite, his smoky glass eyes

on a furred surface—
a line of faces to kiss

at bedtime & who were
the students when I was teacher—

we sat on the floor
as I passed out the notebook

paper I'd cut into columns
to look just like Mrs. Armstrong's.

Each one with a small pencil
(that Dad brought home from golf)—

PT always got 100%
on the spelling quizzes.

Sarah Dickenson Snyder

Bucky was second—one or two words
he'd have to write over 3 times:

experience, experience, experience
necessary, necessary, necessary.

Daniel Suárez

Spanish Inside English

you don't question why Spanish inside English outside you find it normal when you go outside to translate the landscape your parents adopted looking for the way in to and out of one inside you return to comfort the aroma of home an island your feet won't touch you learn too late that Spanish inside English outside means you are outside of who you are inside that you are welcome only so far that your tongue can't cut in line

Jessica Lynn Suchon

Meditation as He Fractures My Collarbone

It is hard to imagine him as broken, not
      breaker, a small boy on his mattress
      in the garage, pressing bruises with his thumb

as he says a prayer for each unbroken
      rib and still hinged socket. His small body
      making myths of his father, building

him up brick by brick the way young
      boys do when their jaw is too splintered
      to form forgiveness. It is hard to imagine

the walls he was thrown through, drywall
      always chalky on his tongue. I wonder
      when it was he first became what he hated,

long before I met him. I hardly think I was
      the first woman he loved with his hands
      wrapped around her throat, skin plum-dark,

capillaries like shattered cathedral glass.
      When he finally stopped and held me, said sorry,
      that he did not know how to love anything – I could

only imagine his mother, framing family photos,
      wanting something to cover all the shadows
      her husband knuckled into the walls.

Brandon Thurman

Something in the Air

It was after the church bonfire
    that my mother's skin
began to change.

        First came the fine spatter
    of red dots seeping
        out into hot blotches.

Then the bulging plump with pus,
    the dozens of rotting grapes & plums
collapsing. It was like a biblical plague:

        inscrutable, cruel. Some queasy,
    wistful part of me wanted
        to touch her misshapen face, to run

my fingers through the stickiness
    of something so loved, so familiar,
changing. For days, she lay naked

        in her locked room, just howling,
    glowering at her impossible clothes.
        We figured some poison ivy

must have vined through the firewood,
    oiled the smoke the praying flames breathed
into the autumn air. If I had to guess,

        I think that must be the closest thing
    to God: this speechless sustenance
        that clouds around our bodies,

shrouds itself in our lungs, sanctifies
     our every whimpering cell—
how we never even notice it

         until it turns. It was around this same time
       that one of my classmates went to sleep
         with his family, not knowing

their furnace had formed a tiny weeping crack.
     I almost said they woke up
dead. Of course, they never woke up at all.

Bevil Townsend

Entropy

You spoke like pain from a jukebox.
The dairy went under. The men sprayed
clean the floor they'd built.

Your whistle and you welding
a smoker. Empty propane tanks
repurposed into pit and stack.

In no acute distress, I watch ants
dismantle a moth wing — its faux eye
powder now. Your exit —

no other changes noted.
The sky — hatched and
unremarkable.

A l e x a n d e r   U l a n o v
translated from the Russian by Alex Cigale

Complete list of things stolen from a burglarized one-room apartment (with complementary commentary)

1. UNIS typewriter (the devil take her, barely touched it twice in the past year, a long time now do all my work on a computer, a good thing too I lent the laptop to a woman friend – that's for sure: if you don't share everything with a friend at the right time, all your possessions will flow to a thief in time – Khayyam was right about this, though the caveat is, it's nicer to share with a female friend);

2. Refracting telescope, small, school issue (now this is truly regrettable. Magnified everything 60x, nevertheless, made the craters of the moon visible. It is pleasant to wander among the constellations – so bright and shiny, the streaming dust. Still it was quite heavy, ten kilograms – the scoundrel forgot about the stand, left it for me of course, but it's impossible to look into a telescope holding it in one's hand. So, neither here nor there. If it comes to it, he'll be able to find a replacement stand);

3. Travel iron, German (a useful thing it was too – with a thermoregulator, a spray nozzle, light – the whole works, incapable of flight only. Will need to keep it in mind – also while traveling. Must search and replace);

4. Azimuth brand backpack (well that's a no-brainer, he had to pack the loot in something. Canvas, 1700 grams; new one, mesh – half a kilo; 1200 grams off my shoulders! Thank you, my friend);

5. Black fake leather jacket (street peddlers in Rome scammed me to the tune of 45,000 lira; ours have much to learn from the Italians – the artistry is lacking, and the hard-sell brutish, so that a customer begins to sense some sort of despondency. The velvet one, that's better, he leaves to me – good taste is no longer in vogue among rogues, apparently);

6. 30 eggs (how the heck did he carry them out? And where to?);

7. Package of cookies, Saray (discount brand, poor soul...);

8. Two cans of green peas (that's almost a kilogram! Better he'd taken more of the clothes. So perhaps he was really starving);

9. Fire safety candles, Sterilin – 5 packages, condoms – 3 packages (scumbag!!!)

10. Chocolate, kilo and a half (all I had – down to the partially eaten bar. A chocolate addict, to boot);

11. Victorinox pocket knife (Dang! Just a blade and a can opener – but I don't need anything more – and it had such a comfortable plastic handle. Light, worn smooth, warm to the touch. And… ah, someone's gift…. Oh well).

(Books, all in place.

Money also – though it wasn't hidden far off.

And they didn't steal that ratty old couch of yours?! You asked.)

Laura Van Prooyen

Imaging Test

the amazing machine
                    my mother's brain

scans the dense fields
                    oh child, you are covered

dirt kicks up behind a wagon
                        and now the girl

will get no pink peppermints

                        the amazing machine
prints lines and numbers

            there is your father
                        in one stroke, a graph

the bulldozer

        clears the land for the highway

here is a tuna casserole
                        here are your children

eating only the crumbled potato chips
                            off the top

your son is now driving big rigs

        your daughter never got off the swings

the amazing machine
                    skips rope

a child tells you your mother is dead

                         here is a braided rug
here is your cousin
                    who died last week

pulling you on a towel
                    across your grandma's floor

you will not stop
                    there, your daughter
no longer has cancer

your grandchild
                    which one? is starting college

soon, your boyfriend
                         will be back at the gas station
washing buses
                    you'll bring him a sandwich

comb his hair
                    this amazing machine

rests on a pillow
                    it's cold in there

Transmitting

Mama, we will die on Jupiter.
My mind is wave
and your memory gives bubbles.

I spoke to her as she did to me,
our words arriving before us, uninvited:
All cats are mangroves.
All mangroves are astronauts.
All cats are astronauts? Indeed!

We talked a world into existence
and peopled it with unknowables.

Thus until.

I'm sure you've noticed how she talks,
the teacher said. Yes, I said,
I name her Poet, Star of My Flesh,
I diagnose Divine.

We have Aphasia, I say to her that night.

Mama, that is a hammock, right?

Yes.

Christopher Warner

Lost Highway

*Thus they depart over dark
waters…* Canto III, Inferno

I dream of Acheron, darkest river
of the nearly damned, and my guide neither
Virgil nor Dante nor Celan, but Ray,
the salted cabbie who once ferried me
across the crumbling vistas of Chicago,
smoking cowboy killers and telling lies
all the way down Cicero while I tried
to find, for the thousandth time, an answer
to Christ's first question according to John —
What do you want? or, *What do you seek?*
I want the wanting, I think, but maybe
that's a cheap trick, as if love were merely
an unrequited thumb on some roadside.
*I was just a lad, nearly twenty-two
Neither good nor bad, just a kid like you…*
Ray hums along and tells me how Hank died
in the back of a Cadillac, empties
rolling on the floor, unfinished lyrics
on the seat. *That's not a bad way to go,*
I say, but I don't mean it, not really,
and Ray says nothing, but checks the meter
and lights another, then looks back and asks
where we're headed, and what I can cover.

July Westhale

Forgiving the Body

This winter slices my weather-proofing as a colicky baby would
        cut air with distemper. I'd stirred only once, to check
the trees, the lines of white birch, perfectly combed as a line
        of cocaine. I acknowledge it is not the wind from Lake Merritt,
which is rapid in multiplication: a lake to the power of itself,

in suspended reflection. Nor the velocity of ice cream trucks,
        ruckus bringing our childhoods to their knees. I have to say
(forgive my frankness), the facts are there. Weather is deniable
        wilderness in California. I needn't tell you I think about
my womb often, a slanted question mark. Walls ridged like someone

clawed couldn't bear to leave. Red every month spelling *vacancy*.
        You'd not bear it, either, waking in the night to soothe a thing
not living, not even conceived of. It's the thoughtlessness, it is.
        At my age, my mother thought of me all of the time. Cupped
with a feeding tube behind her navel base (as if airplanes weren't

all sleeping in some grand ethereal womb, as if we couldn't romanticize
        unimaginable dread)—then the words: bright light, cut away,
latching on, schedule, teething. The thinking becomes not-thinking. Us
        animatronics. She's been asleep in a dirt cradle. Left me
this inheritance. Stronger in Winter than Spring: dead arms branching, branching.

Valentine

The love note wet in my hand; ink erasing itself. The girl is nowhere I'd know how to find her. Moved on or dead. The news on grandpa's old transistor warns that those of us still here should stay indoors for the forseeable future. He admits the future after that is unforeseen. Thick moss brailles up the white picket schoolyard fence. Some newly discovered planet, he boasts, & another that is merely a moon. The principal talks about reinstating the drill. My father says his father never forgot the calm gray expressions on those he killed. There is a box banded to each desk. I have no idea which of us deserves this love.

Katie Willingham

Replica of the Unknown

you get it—cut the thing down to size, a scale model in
    a glass case so you don't

share the same air, and you're laughing now because
    it has dawned on you also

that it was a trap from the start: what careful attention
    to get it right,

exacting as Burton's tome: *melancholy can be overcome only*
    by melancholy. I never claimed

to want the explosive. Give me   a supernatural stomach
    whose acid can dissolve any poison. I took it

as a good omen, this urgency   to explain—
to describe is to crumble, surely,

but like the carrion birds we blamed   for their appetites,
    it was a misrecognition: no one

wanted to point to how many bodies   were left rotting.
    Not for the first time,

I do the laundry   begrudging what I'm wearing
          wanting, if only briefly,

to have everything clean.   Before understanding any beginning
          you have begun to break things,

find yourself   tethered, lit up with intention and
          it doesn't matter

the size of the black box.   Damn, if you don't want to
          put your hand right in it.

Secret

Don't tell, Mama says when I catch her eating the chocolate cake in the middle of the night. Your daddy, he don't need to know. Just gonna make him fret.

My head is a lake. All kinds of boat secrets floating around. Some of them sunk to the lake floor.

I tell Mama, don't worry. Why, just last week, I spent all morning eating the bananas off the stand at Carter's grocery. Just stood there like a burglar monkey, I did.

I don't know why she's keeping all this from Daddy, him being all dead like he is.

We go on like that, me and my mama. The air filled with deadness and chocolate and secrets in the quivering dark.

Genevieve Zimantas

This Border is Guarded by Trees

See the delicately folded feet of road kill, just over
the border along a westward road? Some people don't like corners.
Still, the whole town might be a pocket

tucked into the middle of itself. At the corner store, the neon sign
that used to say "Open," says "pen." Give it ten months
and it will stand on its last leg: for your viewing pleasure,

an "n." It will stay that way for eight years—
this country is young. The thing about somewhere is,
it has a gravity of its own. So cigarette butts flourish

like firecrackers for Victoria Day, when they're flicked
through speeding windows, but only, come to think of it, at night.
And the men stand around in the early evening, a murmuring,

receding gums and worms dragging themselves drowning
from the dirt at their feet—it has not rained
for decades. Two in the lake is worth one in the bucket,

but no one learned to identify birds from the ground.
Mrs. Hursk is infatuated with her best friend's son, but she can fell
and strip a tree in fourteen minutes. Her husband

is teaching himself calculus during dinner, and he picks his teeth
with a knife. Last summer my uncle built a jungle gym out of PVC pipes.
He doesn't trust it yet to bear weight, so I am learning

to fill my days the way summer light fills a punch bowl.
I go walking through woods that know me
by the silence I bring. The crickets, the blackbirds

go quiet. There are only cars and a wizened stand of trees.
They're the frame of this town and its tinder.
You will know me by the skip of the shadows they bring.

Martha Zweig

But No

You might think—but no. There, there,
little glitch. Every mother's morning crust & cuddle
warms to her own oddling infant error.

Factored in, figured out & even then held harmless
in human arms: you might think arms in armories,
inventoried municipal guns & grenades, but no,

just a mother's in loose lime sleeves, a terry robe she tugs
whose hem, wrists & elbows wear & tear
up to her eyes' corners' worntorn tears but no

drone-fired outburst of Afghan weddings spatters unsightly
upon her, & today she's off from a staunch American
cubicle whose papers want their processing but no

one wonders through the manual: not she.
The baby flaps like pennants raising wherever human mettle revs
on notions refreshed during hours of irrational dark, but no

good night's sleep rallies the rest of us much, wee one—
protagonies confabulate among themselves such quests
as somebody ought to have ventured, but no one did or does.

Antipersonnel myself some days, I pray *let it begin*
with me. Our suicide recruiters croon *yes yes!* —but no
still seems to be all I'll give or take for an answer.

CONTRIBUTORS' NOTES

BELLA AKHMADULINA (1937-2010) was a post-Stalinist Soviet Russian poet, most noted for the apolitical character of her writing, uncommon in the Krushchev era, writing instead in an intensely personal manner uniquely masked in classical forms. Her ecstatic reading style in recital made her a literary superstar, along with husband Yevgeny Yevtushenko, capable of filling sports stadiums with adoring fans. In her time, Joseph Brodsky cited her as the best poet living in the Russian language.

DEJAN ALEKSIC, born in 1972, is a Serbian poet, playwright, and author of children's literature. He has published nine poetry books and 15 books for children, which have won him many significant literary awards. His poems and books for children have been translated into several European languages. He lives and works in Kraljevo.

JP ALLEN's poems appear in *Tinderbox, Cactus Heart, After the Pause*, and elsewhere. He is a recent recipient of an MFA in Poetry from Johns Hopkins, and has received scholarships from the Vermont Studio Center and the Sewanee Writers' Conference.

M. J. ARLETT was born in the U.K. and is pursuing her PhD in Texas. She is an editor at the Plath Poetry Project and her work has appeared or is forthcoming in *B O D Y, The Boiler, Lunch Ticket, Poet Lore, Mud Season Review, Rust + Moth*, and elsewhere.

CYRUS ARMAJANI teaches reading and creative writing to incarcerated youth. His poems have appeared in *Berkeley Poetry Review, Blue Collar Review*, and *100 Days Action*, among other publications. *Benefits of Doubt* (Nomadic Press, 2016) is his first book. Cyrus is Iranian-American and lives in Oakland, California, with his wife and two sons.

JULIA ARMSTRONG graduated from Washington College in 2015 with a BA in English and creative writing. In 2017, she received an Individual Artist Grant in poetry from the Maryland State Arts Council. She now works as the administrative assistant for the Rose O'Neill Literary House. This is her first publication.

GABRIELLE BATES is the Social Media Manager of Open Books and a Made at Hugo House fellow. Her work appears in *Poetry Magazine, New England Review*, and the *Best of the Net* anthology, and she helps edit the *Seattle Review, Poetry Northwest*, and *Broadsided Press*. Originally from Birmingham, Alabama, she currently lives in Seattle. gabriellebat.es.

PRITHA BHATTACHARYYA is a Bengali-American writer who received her B.A. from Cornell University. Her work appears or is forthcoming in *Ninth Letter, Crab Orchard Review, The Blueshift Journal, Plain China: Best Undergraduate Writing*, and elsewhere. She serves as a prose reader for *The Adroit Journal*. To learn more, visit prithabread.wordpress.com.

AMY BILODEAU's work has appeared or is forthcoming in *Two Hawks Quarterly, Connotation Press, Monkeybicycle, Sweet: A Literary Confection*, and elsewhere. Her full-length manuscript was a finalist for the 2017 Four Way Books Levis Prize in Poetry. She lives in Bloomington, Indiana.

KAMIL BOUŠKA is a contemporary Czech poet. His first solo collection is *Oheň po slavnosti*, for which he received two nominations for the national Magnesia Litera award, in the Poetry and Discovery of the Year categories. In 2015, he published his second collection of poetry, *Hemisféry* (Fra).

AARON BROWN has been published in *World Literature Today, Tupelo Quarterly, Cimarron Review*, and *Transition*, among others. A collection of poetry, *Acacia Road*, is the winner of the 2016 Gerald Cable Book Award (Silverfish Review Press). Brown grew up in Chad and now lives in Kansas, where he is a professor of writing at Sterling College.

DEZIREÉ A. BROWN is a black queer woman poet, scholar and social justice warrior, born and raised in Flint, Michigan. An MFA candidate at Northern Michigan University, work by this poet has appeared or is forthcoming in *BOATT, decomP, Cartridge Lit*, and *The Boiler*, among others. Tweeting at @deziree_a_brown.

ANNAH BROWNING hails from the foothills of South Carolina, but now calls Chicago home. She holds an MFA from Washington University in St. Louis and a PhD from the Program for Writers at The University of Illinois-Chicago, and she is the author of a chapbook, *The Marriage* (Horse Less Press, 2013). Her poems have recently appeared in *Black Warrior Review, Southern Indiana Review, Midwestern Gothic*, and elsewhere. She is poetry editor of *Grimoire*, an online literary magazine of dark arts.

ERIKA BRUMETT's words appear in numerous journals, including *North American Review, Prairie Schooner*, and *The Los Angeles Review*. She earned Honorable Mention for the 2017 James Hurst Poetry Prize, and her novel, *Scrap Metal Sky*, was published in 2016 by Shape&Nature Press.

RICK BURSKY lives in Los Angeles. His most recent book, *I'm No Longer Troubled by the Extravagance*, is out from BOA Editions; his previous book, *Death Obscura*, was published by Sarabande Books. He teaches poetry for the Writer's Program at UCLA Extension.

BISCUITS CALHOUN used to be someone else and, often, still is. He is currently at work on an essay about Dissociative Identity Disorder (DID); a full-length poetry collection, *What Is Who*, will be out in 2018 from Spuyten Duyvil. He plays drums in Shitty Band and manages Mussel in Austin, Texas, where he lives with his wife and their puppy dog. More at biscuitscalhoun.com.

JOHN RANDOLPH CARTER is a poet and artist, finalist in the *National Poetry Series*. He has poetry in journals including *Barrow Street, Cream City Review, LIT, North American Review, Sewanee Review, Verse, Verse Daily*, and *Western Humanities Review*. He is a recipient of NEA, New York State Council, and Fulbright grants, and has art in 32 public collections including the Metropolitan Museum of Art. johnrandolphcarter.blogspot.com.

SUSANA H. CASE is the author of five books of poetry, most recently, *Drugstore Blue*, from Five Oaks Press, and *4 Rms w Vu*, from Mayapple Press, as well as four chapbooks. She is a Professor and Program Coordinator at the New York Institute of Technology in New York City.

CORTNEY LAMAR CHARLESTON is the author of *Telepathologies* (Saturnalia Books, 2017). A recipient of fellowships from Cave Canem, The Conversation Literary Festival, and the New Jersey State Council on the Arts, his poems have appeared in *Poetry, New England Review, Gulf Coast, TriQuarterly, 32 Poems*, and elsewhere.

GEET CHATURVEDI is a Hindi poet and novelist. He has authored six books, including two books of novellas and two poetry books. The novella *Simsim* won a PEN/Heim Grant. His poems have been translated into seventeen languages. He was awarded the Bharat Bhushan Agrawal Award (poetry) and Krishna Pratap Award (fiction).

ALEX CIGALE's own English-language poems have appeared in *The Common, Colorado*, and *The Literary Reviews*, and his translations in *Harvard Review, The Hopkins Review, Kenyon Review, New England Review, Modern Poetry in Translation, TriQuarterly, Words Without Borders*, and *World Literature Today*. He was awarded the 2015 NEA Translation Fellowship for his work on Mikhail Eremin. His first full book, *Russian Absurd: Daniil Kharms, Selected Writings*, is just out in the Northwestern World Classics series.

ALBERT DeGENOVA is an award-winning poet, editor, teacher, and blues saxophonist. He is the author of three books of poetry and three chapbooks. In June 2000 he launched the literary/arts journal *After Hours*; he continues as publisher and co-editor. DeGenova received his MFA in Writing from Spalding University, Louisville.

BRYCE EMLEY is a freelancer, editor, and barista in New Mexico. His poetry and prose can be found in *The Atlantic, Narrative, Boston Review, Prairie Schooner, Best American Experimental Writing*, and he serves as Poetry Editor of *Raleigh Review*. Read more at bryceemley.com.

E. J. EVANS is a poet and musician living in Cazenovia, New York. His poetry has appeared in many literary journals including *Stone Canoe, Confrontation, Poetry East*, and *Rattle*. His poetry chapbook, *First Snow Coming*, was published by Kattywompus Press. He is currently at work on a prose-poem collection.

JOSEPH FASANO is the author of three books of poetry: *Vincent* (Cider Press, 2015); *Inheritance* (2014), a James Laughlin Award nominee; and *Fugue for Other Hands* (2013), which won the Cider Press Review Book Award and was nominated by Linda Pastan for the Poets Prize, "awarded annually for the best book of verse published by a living American poet in the two years prior to the award year." His poems and essays have appeared in *The Yale Review, The Southern Review, The Missouri Review, The Times Literary Supplement, Tin House*, and other publications. A winner of the *Rattle* Poetry Prize, he teaches at Manhattanville College and Columbia University, where he is also the Faculty Advisor for *Quarto*.

VICTORIA C. FLANAGAN is the Lead Associate Editor Emerita for *Blackbird*. She is the recipient of the Catherine and Joan Byrne Poetry Prize from the Academy of American Poets and an MFA scholarship to the Sewanee Writers' Conference. Her poetry is forthcoming in *Beloit Poetry Journal*.

RICKY GARNI has worked over the years as a teacher, wine merchant, composer, and graphic designer. His poetry has been nominated for the Pushcart Prize on seven occasions and is widely available on the Web. His latest work, *VIA*, was slated for release in late 2017.

ANITA GOPALAN is a PEN/Heim Translation Grant awardee. Her translated poetry chapbook, *Ants in the Book*, is an Anomalous Press finalist. Her work has appeared in *World Literature Today, Poetry International, Two Lines, Asymptote, the PEN America*, and *Modern Poetry in Translation*. She serves as a member of the PEN Translation Committee.

SAMANTHA GRENROCK received an MFA from the University of Florida, and her work has appeared or is forthcoming in *New Orleans Review, Horsethief, Raritan, Best New Poets*, and other journals. She is the winner of the 2017 Robert and Adele Schiff Award in poetry from *The Cincinnati Review*.

BENJAMIN S. GROSSBERG's work includes *Space Traveler* (University of Tampa, 2014), *Sweet Core Orchard* (University of Tampa, 2009), winner of the Tampa Review Prize and a Lambda Literary Award, and the chapbook, *An Elegy* (Jacar Press, 2016). Grossberg works as Director of Creative Writing at the University of Hartford.

JACKLEEN HOLTON HOOKWAY's poems have appeared in the anthologies *The Giant Book of Poetry* and *Steve Kowit: This Unspeakably Marvelous Life*, and in journals including *Atlanta Review, Bayou, Bellingham Review, North American Review, Poet Lore, Rattle*, and *Slipstream*.

AMANDA GALVAN HUYNH is a Chicana poet living in New York. She is the recipient of scholarships from the Sewanee Conference and Sundress Academy for the Arts. In 2016, her poem was selected for the AWP Intro Journal Project Award. Her work has appeared in *Muzzle Magazine, Tahoma Literary Review*, and others.

LUISA A. IGLORIA is the winner of the inaugural 2015 Resurgence Prize for Poetry (U.K.) and the author of *Ode to the Heart Smaller than a Pencil Eraser* (2014 May Swenson Prize) and other works. She is on the faculty of the MFA Creative Writing Program at Old Dominion University. luisaigloria.com.

MARLIN M. JENKINS was born and raised in Detroit and studied poetry in University of Michigan's MFA program. His writings have been given homes by *The Collagist*, *The Journal*, and *Bennington Review*, among others. He is an editor for HEArt Online, and you can find him on Twitter @Marlin_Poet.

MARCI RAE JOHNSON's poems appear in *The Collagist*, *Quiddity*, *Hobart*, *Redivider*, *Redactions*, *The Louisville Review*, and *32 Poems*, among others. Her first collection of poetry was published by Sage Hill Press in 2013, and her second collection, *Basic Disaster Supplies Kit*, was released by Steel Toe Books in 2016.

SARAH JORDAN is a writer based in New York. Her work has or will appear in *the minnesota review*, *Cosmonauts Avenue*, *Souvenir Lit*, *Entropy Magazine*, and others. She occasionally tweets @sajordan01.

VLADISLAV KHODASEVICH, a prominent Russian poet, translator of poetry, a writer and critic, was born in Moscow in 1886 and died in Paris in 1939. He is the author of seminal books about the great Russian poets Derzhavin and Pushkin. His poetry was praised by Innokenty Annensky, Valery Briusov, and Vladimir Nabokov, who brilliantly translated Khodasevich's "Ballata." Khodasevich published five books of poetry in his lifetime, *Heavy Lyre* being the last one published in Russia, later reprinted in Berlin. After wandering in Europe (Germany, Italy, London, Dublin), he finally settled in Paris, where he became a leading literary critic.

PATRICK KINDIG is a PhD candidate in Indiana University's Department of English. He is the author of the micro-chapbook *Dry Spell* (Porkbelly Press 2016), and his poems have recently appeared in *CutBank*, *Meridian*, *Third Coast*, *Hobart*, *Muzzle*, and other journals.

ADIE SMITH KLECKNER lives among piles of books with her husband, daughter, and dog. She studied poetry and visual art at Belhaven University and received an MFA in poetry from Seattle Pacific University. Her work has appeared in *Cutthroat*, *Structo*, and *Ruminate*, among others. She recently moved to Tacoma, Washington, and teaches at Green River College. In her poetry, she finds herself returning to the timelessness of leaving and returning from war, and the people who are left in the wake.

VIRGINIA KONCHAN is the author of a poetry collection, *The End of Spectacle* (Carnegie Mellon, 2018), a collection of short stories, *Anatomical Gift* (Noctuary Press, 2017), and two chapbooks. Co-founder of *Matter* and Associate Editor for *Tupelo Quarterly*, she teaches at Marist College.

BRANDON KRIEG is the author of two poetry collections, *In the Gorge* (Codhill Press, 2017) and *Invasives* (New Rivers Press, 2014). He lives in Columbia, Missouri, and teaches at Westminster College.

KIMBERLY KRUGE is the author of *Ordinary Chaos* (CMU Press, 2018) and the chapbook *High-Land Sub-Tropic*, which won the 2017 Center for Book Arts Prize. Her poems have appeared in *Ploughshares, The Iowa Review, Copper Nickel, The Denver Quarterly*, and elsewhere. She lives and works in Guadalajara, Mexico.

ROSA LANE is author of *Tiller North* (Sixteen Rivers Press), winner of a 2017 National Indie Excellence Award and 2017 Maine Literary Award, and *Roots and Reckonings*, a chapbook. Rosa received her MFA from Sarah Lawrence College. Her poems have appeared in *Crab Orchard Review, New South, Ploughshares*, and *Verse Daily*.

HEATHER KIRN LANIER is the author of two award-winning poetry chapbooks, *The Story You Tell Yourself* (Kent State, 2012) and *Heart-Shaped Bed in Hiroshima* (Standing Rock Cultural Arts, 2015). Her memoir about raising a child with a rare chromosomal condition is forthcoming from Penguin Press.

BRENNA LEMIEUX is the author of two collections of poetry, *The Gospel of Household Plants* and *Blankness, Melancholy, and Other Ways of Dying*. She lives in Chicago with her husband.

MAJA LUKIC is a poet and environmental attorney. Her work has appeared or is forthcoming in *Colorado Review, Prelude, Salamander, Sugar House Review, Vinyl, Posit, Canary*, and other journals. Selected pieces published online are available at majalukic.com, and she can be found on Twitter: @majalukic113. She lives in New York City.

ANGIE MACRI is the author of *Underwater Panther* (Southeast Missouri State University), winner of the Cowles Poetry Book Prize, and *Fear Nothing of the Future or the Past* (Finishing Line). Her recent work appears in *Bluestem, New Madrid*, and *Quiddity*. An Arkansas Arts Council fellow, she lives in Hot Springs.

JENNIFER MANTHEY is an MFA student at Hamline University in St Paul, Minnesota. She has served as Assistant Poetry Editor for the *Water~Stone Review* and is a current Associate Editor for *Runestone Journal*. Her work has appeared recently in journals such as *Crab Orchard Review, Rise Up Review*, and *Literary Mama*, and has been nominated for a Pushcart Prize in poetry.

MAYA MARSHALL is an editor, writer, and poet. She is the author of the chapbook *Secondhand* (2016, Dancing Girl Press) and holds fellowships from Callaloo and Cave Canem.

DIANE G. MARTIN, Russian literature specialist and graduate of Willamette University, has published writing and photographs in numerous journals, including *New London Writers, Poetry Circle, Conclave*, and *Slipstream*. She is currently finishing a collection of short stories and essays. Widely traveled, Diane's major themes are exile, disability, and reluctant nomadism.

PETAR MATOVIĆ was born in 1978 (Serbia, Požega). He has published four poetry books: *Kamerni komadi* (Chamber Pieces, 1997); *Koferi Džima Džarmuša* (Suitcases of Jim Jarmusch, 2009 — also published as *Walizki Jima Jarmusha*, Poland, 2011; *Les maletes de Jim Jarmusch*, Spain, 2013); *Odakle dolaze dabrovi* (Where the Beavers Come From, 2013); *Iz srećne republike* (From the Happy Republic, 2017).

IULIA MILITARU is Chief Editor of frACTalia Press and *InterRe:ACT* magazine. Her first poetry collection *Marea Pipeadă* (The Great Pipe Epic) was published in 2010, receiving two major awards. *Dramadoll*, co-authored with Anca Bucur and Cristina Florentina Budar, is part of a larger poetry/graphic art/video/sound project. The video *Images of the day number 8*, directed by Cristina Florentina Budar, was selected in *Gesamt 2012 (DISASTER 501 What happened to man?)*, coordinated by Lars von Trier and directed by Jenle Hallund. Her collection of experimental poetry *Confiscarea bestiei (o postcercetare)* (The Seizure of the Beast. A Post-research) was published by frACTalia Press in 2016. She published poems and digital collages in *MAINTENANT, A Journal of Contemporary Dada Writing and Art (#9-11)*, and her art show "The Path. Filling-in Abstract Forms: Overwriting Barnett Newman" opened at Public Space One, Iowa City, 2016. In 2016, she participated in The Third Annual Brussels *Poetry Fest*.

PAMELA MILLER is a Chicago poet whose work has appeared in *RHINO, Peacock Journal, Pirene's Fountain, New Poetry from the Midwest 2017, Star 82 Review, MAYDAY*, and elsewhere. She has published four books of poetry, most recently *Miss Unthinkable* (Mayapple Press, 2013), and is working on a new collection.

NICOLE MIYASHIRO writes poetry and fiction and supports literary programs with the Pennsylvania Center for the Book at Penn State University. Her work appears in *The Dr. T. J. Eckleburg Review, Four Chambers*, the anthology *Nasty Women Poets: An Unapologetic Anthology of Subversive Verse* (Lost Horse Press), and elsewhere.

FAISAL MOHYUDDIN is the author of *The Displaced Children of Displaced Children* (Eyewear Publishing, 2018), winner of the 2017 Sexton Prize, and the chapbook *The Riddle of Longing* (Backbone Press, 2017). The recipient of the 2014 Edward Stanley Award from *Prairie Schooner* and a 2017 Gwendolyn Brooks Poetry Prize, he serves as an educator adviser to Narrative 4 and teaches English at Highland Park High School in Illinois.

CHESWAYO MPHANZA was born in Lusaka, Zambia, and raised in Chicago. His work has been featured in, or is forthcoming from, *New England Review, Vinyl, Prairie Schooner, Hayden's Ferry Review*, and *RHINO*. He has received fellowships from the Bread Loaf Writers Conference, Callaloo, Columbia University, and Cave Canem. He is currently an MFA candidate in poetry at Rutgers-Newark.

ELISABETH MURAWSKI is the author of *Zorba's Daughter*, which won the May Swenson Poetry Award, *Moon and Mercury*, and two chapbooks, *Troubled by an Angel* and *Out-patients*. Publications include *The Yale Review, The Hudson Review, FIELD*, et al. A native of Chicago, she currently lives in Alexandria, Virginia.

AMANDA MURPHY has written two collections of poetry, *The Lost Lines* and *Portland*. She enjoys writing about mythology and small-town folklore, cyclic patterns, and loss. She and her husband live in Indiana. They have a baby and a Maine Coon cat. The cat is the larger of the two.

ABBY E. MURRAY teaches creative writing at the University of Washington Tacoma and is the editor of *Collateral*, a literary journal that showcases writing about the impact of war and military service beyond the combat zone. Her recent poems have been published in *Rattle*, *Prairie Schooner*, and *Rise Up Review*.

AMANDA NEWELL's recent work has appeared or is forthcoming in *Bellevue Literary Review*, *North American Review*, *Scoundrel Time*, *storySouth*, and elsewhere. She holds an MFA in poetry from Warren Wilson College and teaches at The Gunston School on Maryland's Eastern Shore.

ELIZABETH O'BRIEN is the recipient of a Minnesota Emerging Writers' Grant through the Loft Literary Center, and the James Wright Poetry Award from the Academy of American Poets. Her writing has appeared in many magazines and anthologies, including *New England Review*, *The Rumpus*, *Tin House*, *Best New Poets 2016*, *Radar Poetry*, *Ploughshares*, and AWP's *Writer's Chronicle*. She lives in Minneapolis.

ALISON A. OGUNMOKUN is a writer, comedian, and MFA candidate at the University of California in San Diego. She was the co-curator of a Live Lit show in Chicago that featured women and non-binary artists called "Spread Your Own Gossip."

PAUL OTREMBA is the author of two poetry collections, *Pax Americana* (Four Way Books, 2015) and *The Currency* (Four Way Books, 2009). He teaches at Rice University and in the low-residency MFA program at Warren Wilson College.

ONDŘEJ PAZDÍREK is a Czech-American writer and translator. He's the winner of the 2017 Beacon Street Prize in poetry from *Redivider*. His work has recently appeared in *Poet Lore*, *Phoebe*, *Guernica*, and *Two Lines*, and is forthcoming from *Southern Humanities Review*, *PANK*, *Gulf Coast*, and *Hayden's Ferry Review*, among others.

TRENTON POLLARD is a queer poet who lives in Queens, and is a Teaching Fellow at Columbia University. Recent work has been published or is forthcoming in *Passages North*, *Bennington Review*, *North American Review*, *Denver Quarterly*, *Lambda Literary*, and elsewhere.

IAN PROBSTEIN, associate professor of English at Touro College, has published 10 books of poetry, translated a dozen poetry volumes and anthologies of poetry in translation; in all, he has about 500 publications. His most recent book is *The River of Time: Time-Space, Language and History in Avant-Garde, Modernist, and Contemporary Poetry* (Boston: Academic Studies Press, 2017).

DOUG RAMSPECK is the author of six poetry collections and one collection of short stories. His most recent book, *Black Flowers*, is forthcoming from LSU Press. Individual poems have appeared in journals that include *The Southern Review, Kenyon Review, Slate*, and *The Georgia Review*.

FRANCISCO LAYNA RANZ is a poet, editor and literary critic who lives in Madrid, Spain. He has taught Spanish literature at universities in Spain and the U.S., and has published three scholarly books on medieval and Golden Age Spanish literature. He is the author of two books of poems: *Y una sospecha, como un dedo* (Amargord, 2016) and *Espíritu, hueso animal* (RIL Editores, 2017).

KIMBERLY REYES has received fellowships from the Poetry Foundation, Columbia University, and San Francisco State University. Her chapbook *Warning Coloration* is forthcoming from Dancing Girl Press.

MERLIN URAL RIVERA's writing has appeared in *Rattle, Natural Bridge, Warscapes* and *Hot Street*, among other journals. Born in Bulgaria and raised in Turkey, she now lives in New Jersey and teaches writing and literature at the School of Visual Arts.

R. FLOWERS RIVERA is a Mississippi native who now lives in McKinney, Texas. Her second collection of poetry, *Heathen* (Wayne State, 2015), was selected as the winner of the 2015 Naomi Long Madgett Poetry Award as well as the 2016 Mississippi Institute of Arts and Letters Poetry Award. Rivera's debut collection of poetry, *Troubling Accents* (Xavier Review Press, 2013), received a nomination from the Mississippi Institute of Arts and Letters and was selected by the Texas Association of Authors as its 2014 Poetry Book of the Year. Dr. Rivera has a PhD from Binghamton University, MA from Hollins University, MS from Georgia State University, and a BS from The University of Georgia.

ILIANA ROCHA earned her PhD in English Literature-Creative Writing from Western Michigan University. Her work has been featured in the *Best New Poets 2014* anthology, as well as *Bennington Review, Blackbird*, and *West Branch*. *Karankawa*, her debut collection, won the 2014 AWP Donald Hall Prize for Poetry.

ERIC ROY has poetry recently published in *Spillway, Green Mountains Review, Souvenir Lit*, and *the minnesota review*. He has won awards for his teaching (Teacher of the Year - Virginia College, Austin 2014), chili (13th Annual ACCA Cook-Off - 1st Place), and poetry (2015 KGB Open 'After the AWP' Winner).

AUSTIN SANCHEZ-MORAN received his MFA in Poetry from George Mason University. His poems and short fiction have been published or are forthcoming in *The Laurel Review, Denver Quarterly*, and *Salamander Magazine*, among many others. Also, he had a poem chosen for the anthology, *Best New Poets of the Midwest* (2017).

CLAUDIA SEREA's poems and translations have appeared in *Field, New Letters, Meridian, Word Riot, Apple Valley Review,* and many others. An eight-time Pushcart Prize and four-time Best of the Net nominee, she is the author of *Angels & Beasts* (Phoenicia Publishing, 2012), *A Dirt Road Hangs From the Sky* (8th House Publishing, 2013), *To Part Is to Die a Little* (Cervena Barva Press, 2015) and *Nothing Important Happened Today* (Broadstone Books, 2016). Serea co-hosts The Williams Readings poetry series in Rutherford, New Jersey, and is a co-founder and editor of *National Translation Month*. More at cserea.tumblr.com

HILARY SIDERIS is the author of *Most Likely to Die* (Poets Wear Prada, 2014) and *The Inclination to Make Waves* (Big Wonderful, 2016). She lives in Brooklyn and works for The City University of New York. She has a BA in English literature from Indiana University and an MFA from the University of Iowa Writers' Workshop.

VOLKER SIELAFF was born in 1966 and lives in Dresden, Germany. His poems, essays and criticism have appeared widely, and his poems have been translated into ten different languages. His work was included in the anthology *Twentieth Century German Poetry*, published by Farrar, Straus and Giroux (New York, 2005), and his collection of poetry, *Postkarte für Nofretete*, was awarded the Lessing Prize in 2005.

CHARLES SIMIC's work has won numerous awards, among them the 1990 Pulitzer Prize, the MacArthur Foundation "genius grant," the Griffin International Poetry Prize, and, simultaneously, the Wallace Stevens Award and appointment as U.S. Poet Laureate. He taught English and creative writing for over thirty years at the University of New Hampshire. Although he emigrated to the U.S. from Yugoslavia as a teenager, Simic writes in English, drawing upon his own experiences of war-torn Belgrade to compose poems about the physical and spiritual poverty of modern life.

SARAH DICKENSON SNYDER has two poetry collections, *The Human Contract* and *Notes from a Nomad*. Poems have appeared recently in *The Comstock Review, Damfino Press, The Main Street Rag, Chautauqua Literary Magazine, Piedmont Journal, Sunlight Press, Stirring: a Literary Journal,* and *Whale Road Review.*

VESNA STAMENKOVIĆ was born in Belgrade in 1977, studied Spanish language and Hispanic literatures, and has been translating literary prose and poetry from and to Serbian, English, Spanish, and Portuguese, for various publishers and literary magazines in Serbia and abroad. She is a member of the Managing Board of the Association of Literary Translators of Serbia.

DANIEL SUÁREZ is a first generation Cuban American born and raised in Chicago. His poems can be found in *The Columbia Poetry Review, Eleven Eleven, 5x5, Borderlands: Texas Poetry Review,* and other journals.

JESSICA LYNN SUCHON lives in Nashville. She received her MFA from Southern Illinois University where she was recognized by The Academy of American Poets. Jessica was named a 2016 Emerging Writer Fellow by Aspen Words and was a finalist for the 2017 Indiana Review Prize.

MARK TERRILL is an American poet, writer and translator living in Germany since 1984. His translations of Günter Grass, Peter Handke, Rolf Dieter Brinkmann, Jörg Fauser, Nicolas Born, Silke Scheuermann, and others have appeared in many journals, as well as in several full-length collections, chapbooks, and broadsides. He was guest editor for the German Poetry edition of the *Atlanta Review* (Volume XV, Issue Number 2, 2009).

BRANDON THURMAN is the author of the chapbook *Strange Flesh* (Quarterly West, 2018). His poetry can be found in *Nashville Review, Ninth Letter, The Journal, PANK, The Blueshift Journal*, and others. He lives in Fayetteville, Arkansas, with his husband and son. You can find him online at brandonthurman.com.

BEVIL TOWNSEND's work, formerly published in the name of Ellie Tipton, has appeared or is forthcoming in *North American Review, Forklift Ohio*, and *Zone3*, among other places. She formerly taught writing at The University of Maryland and is currently a freelance writer, editor, and archiver for Campaign Greenhouse in Washington, D.C..

ALEXANDER ULANOV lives in Samara and works at Samara State Aerospace University. His books of poetry are *Wind Direction* (1990), *Dry Light* (1993), *Waves and Ladders* (1997), *Displacements +* (2007), *Methods of Seeing* (2012), and the book of prose *Between We* (2006). He received the Andrey Bely prize for his criticism (2009). Alex Cigale's other translations of Ulanov's prose poems have appeared in *Bat City Review, Fourteen Hills, The Manhattan Review, Plume, Southeast Review, Talisman*, and *Washington Square Review*.

LAURA VAN PROOYEN is author of two collections of poetry, *Our House Was on Fire* (Ashland Poetry Press, 2015) and *Inkblot and Altar* (Pecan Grove Press, 2006). She teaches in the low-residency MFA Creative Writing program at Miami University in Oxford, Ohio, and lives in San Antonio, Texas.

JESSICA L. WALSH is the author of two poetry collections, *How to Break My Neck* (ELJ) and *Banished* (Red Paint Hill) as well as two chapbooks. Her work has appeared recently in *Tinderbox, Midwestern Gothic, Glass, Rogue Agent*, and more. She has been nominated for the Pushcart Prize, Best New Poets, and Bettering American Poetry, and was also honored to receive a second place award in the 2014 Illinois Emerging Poets Competition.

CHRISTOPHER WARNER's poems have appeared or are forthcoming in *Atlanta Review, Drunken Boat, Salamander, Slipstream, Spoon River Poetry Review*, and elsewhere. He works as a brakeman for Union Pacific Railroad and lives in central Illinois with his wife and three boys.

JULY WESTHALE is the author of *Trailer Trash* (2016 Kore Press Book Award), *The Cavalcade*, and the children's book *Occasionally Accurate Science*. Her recent poetry can be found in *The National Poetry Review, Tupelo Quarterly*, and *Quarterly West*. Her essays have been nominated for *Best American Essays*, as well as the Pushcart Prize. She moonlights as a journalist at *The Establishment*, and has appeared in *The Huffington Post*. julywesthale.com.

JOHN SIBLEY WILLIAMS is the author of two poetry collections, most recently *Disinheritance*. A seven-time Pushcart nominee and winner of various awards, John serves as editor of *The Inflectionist Review*. Publications include: *Yale Review, Atlanta Review, Prairie Schooner, Midwest Quarterly, Sycamore Review, Massachusetts Review, Columbia, Third Coast*, and *Poetry Northwest*.

KATIE WILLINGHAM is the author of *Unlikely Designs* (University of Chicago Press, 2017). Her poems have appeared in such publications as *Bennington Review, Kenyon Review, Poem-a-Day, The Journal*, and others. You can find her in person most of the time in Brooklyn, New York, and online always at katiewillingham.com.

FRANCINE WITTE is the author of the poetry chapbooks *Only, Not Only* (Finishing Line Press, 2012) and *First Rain* (Pecan Grove Press, 2009 — winner of the Pecan Grove Press competition), and the flash fiction chapbooks *Cold June* (Ropewalk Press — selected by Robert Olen Butler as winner of the 2010 Thomas A. Wilhelmus Award) and *The Wind Twirls Everything* (MuscleHead Press). Her latest poetry chapbook, *Not All Fires Burn the Same*, won the 2016 Slipstream chapbook contest. She lives in New York City.

GENEVIEVE ZIMANTAS holds an MPhil in modern and contemporary literature from the University of Cambridge, where she worked on Jean Rhys' early novels. Her poems have appeared in journals across Canada and the United States, most recently *Prairie Fire, ARC Poetry Magazine*, and *Contemporary Verse 2*. She lives in Montreal.

MARTHA ZWEIG's collections include *Monkey Lightning* (Tupelo Press, 2010), *What Kind* (Wesleyan University Press, 2003), *Vinegar Bone* (Wesleyan University Press, 1999), and *Powers* (Vermont Arts Council, 1976). *Get Lost*, winner of the 2014 Rousseau Prize, is forthcoming from The National Poetry Review Press/Dream Horse Press.

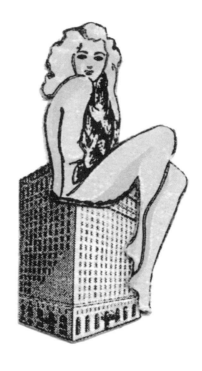

DONORS

Tony Adler

Howard & Jane Alt

John C. Amen

Michael Anderson

Phillip Bimstein

Jan Bottiglieri

Silvia Bonilla

Ann Brandon

Prudence Brown

Debra Bruce

Robin Chapman

Jo Cohlmeyer & Maggie Edgar

Patricia Ann Cogen

Mary Davis & Ron Sherman

Albert DeGenova

Charles & Donna Dickinson

Kimberly Dixon-Mays

Barbara Eaton

John & Carol Eding

David Eingorn

David & Donna Sue Fish

Bill Floyd

Peter & Mary Fritzell

Jan Frodesen

Gail Goepfert

Barbara J. Goldberg

Richard & Janet Goldberg

Ralph Hamilton

Rev. David & Andrea Handley

Nancy Heggem

Ann Hudson

Susan Huebner

Tim Hunt

Kate Hutchinson

David & Rochelle Jones

Richard Jones

Sarah Jordan

Donald Judson

Alfred Klinger

Darlene & Ludwig Krammer

Ruth Kravitz

Michael Lenehan & Mary William

Jane Levine & Randy Signor

Jim & Nancy Litke

Ronald Litke

Ken & Cathy Lomasney

Mike Matheson

Robert McCamant

Donald Meckley & Rose Parisi

Ann Merritt

Michael Miner & Betsy Nore

Michael L. Miner

Annie Moldafsky

Larry Nesper

Erik Norbie

Onyons, Inc.

Liz Peterson

Roger Pfingston

Frances & Philip Podulka

Marcia Pradzinski

Elizabeth Quigg

Jenene Ravesloot & Tom Roby IV

Robert Rohm

Debora Nodler Rosen

Ann Roubal

Carol Sadtler

Jacob Saenz

Nina Sandlin

Dianne Sawyer & David Lipkin

Maureen Seaton

Lee Sharkey

Andrea Witzke Slot

Jon Snider

Jessica Spring

Linda & George Stevenson

Chris Stoessal

Moira Sullivan

Neil Tesser

Herbert K. Tjossem

Michael Tobin

Jill Toffoli

Nick Tryling

University of Wynwood

Sara & Ken Vaux

Valerie Wallace

Frank & Tambra White

Mary K. Young

Marcia Zuckerman

Claim Your Cloudbank Prize
Two awarded each year

A $200 prize is awarded for one poem or flash fiction
in an issue of Cloudbank.

A $1000 prize, plus publication, is awarded for a full-length
manuscript submitted for the Vern Rutsala Book Contest.

Visit cloudbankbooks.com
for contest and submission guidelines.

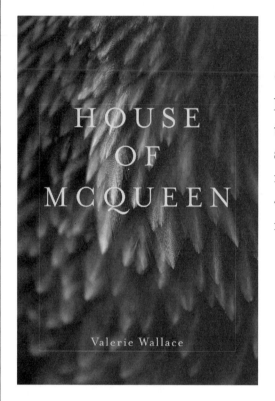

"Wallace conducts a literary seance in her transcendent debut, serving as a scholar and medium . . ."
~ *Publishers Weekly*, starred review

"...I may be tough & selfish but what
Do you expect? I think with my bare hands."
from "Needles"

Selected by Vievee Francis for the Four Way Books Intro Prize, Valerie Wallace's HOUSE OF MCQUEEN is a glittering debut by an assured new voice... At turns fierce and vulnerable, here is a collection that leaps from runway to fairytale to street with wild, brilliant grace.

Available at fourwaybooks.com or wherever books are sold.